Deep Learning for Everyone

Ideas and Impact

FIRST EDITION

Dr. S. DHANASEKARAN

Dr. K. RAJESHKUMAR

Dr. S. KRISHNANARAYANANAN

979-8-8963-2677-9

Notion Press

First Edition: December 2024

AUTHOR PROFILE

Dr. S. Dhanasekaran was born on 16-06-1983 to Mr.P.Subbiah B.Sc., TNEB (Rtd) and Mrs.M.Govindammal Teacher (Rtd) at Mangapuram, Srivilliputtur in Virudhunagar District. He had completed his schooling SSLC & HSC in the year 1998 & 2000 respectively from Mangapuram Hindu Nadar Higher Secondary School, Srivilliputtur. He had finished his Under Graduate Degree, B.E., in Computer Science and Engineering from Madurai Kamarajar University, Tamilnadu, with first class in the year 2004. He has received Post Graduate Degree M.E., (CSE) in First class with Distinction from Annamalai University, Tamilnadu in the year 2007. He secured school first rank in both SSLC & HSC. Dr.S.Dhanasekaran has started his Academic career as Lecturer in Department of IT in Arulmigu Kalasalingam College of Engineering (AKCE) in 2008. Now he is working as Associate Professor & Head in the Department of Information Technology, Kalasalingam University. He has completed Ph.D., (Cloud Computing) in the year 2017 at Kalasalingam University under the Guidance of Dr.V.Vasudevan Senior Professor & Registrar of Kalasalingam University, Srivilliputtur, and Tamilnadu, India. He is highly motivated, well-disciplined professional with 17-years of Teaching Experience in the area of Computer science & Engineering with flexibility, loyalty & strong motivational skills. He is a Life time member of ISTE and IEEE. During these 17-Years of Teaching Experience he has completed many IIT-NPTEL Online Certification course to enrich research knowledge. He has received Best Research paper Award, Teaching Competence Award, Faculty Advisor ship Award and Motivational Awards for 100%Attendance in the Academic Year (2015-16) (2016-17) at Kalasalingam University. He have actively contributed in various Academic, Administrative (UGC, AICTE , NAAC ,ABET, NBA), Research, Placement, and Extension related activities for the growth of Kalasalingam University. He acted as a Resource person and convener for conducting various FDP, Conference, and Workshops. Moreover he has published more than 100 Research papers in which Scopus - (50) and SCI with Impact Factor (Thomson Reuters-(30) Indexed Journals with Impact Factor. Currently He is guiding 7 Ph.D., Scholars in various Research domains and 5 Research Scholars completed their Ph.D., under his Guidance. He is acting as Doctoral Committee (DC) Member for 20 Research Scholars in Anna University. He acted as Indian Examiner Expert for conducting Ph.D., Viva Voce Examination. He has written 4 Text Books and 8 Patents are granted.

Dr. K. Rajeshkumar has a distinguished academic and professional background in the field of electronics, communication, and network engineering. He began his educational journey by completing his Bachelor of Engineering (B.E.) in Electronics and Communication Engineering in 2006. He further advanced his expertise by obtaining a Master of Technology (M.Tech) in Network Engineering in 2010. Demonstrating a commitment to continuous learning, Dr. Rajeshkumar earned his CCNA certification in 2016. Dr. Rajeshkumar commenced his teaching career as an Assistant Professor at Theni Kammavar Sangam College of Technology, located in Theni, Tamil Nadu. Currently, he is working as Assistant Professor in SRM Institute of Science and Tecnology, Kattankulathur, Chennai, Tamil Nadu. Over the course of 14 years, he has made significant contributions to academia, providing guidance to undergraduate students on their projects and encouraging them to pursue international certification courses. He is known for his ability to inspire and motivate students to achieve their academic and professional goals. In 2024, Dr. Rajeshkumar completed his Ph.D. in Big Data Analytics under the mentorship of Dr. S. Dhanasekeran, Associate Professor and Head of the Department of Information Technology at Kalasalingam Academy of Research and Education, Srivilliputhur, Viruthunagar, Tamil Nadu.

Dr. Rajeshkumar's dedication to education is evident in his active participation in academic activities and his unwavering encouragement of students. His philosophy of lifelong learning is reflected in his motto: "Keep Learning always".

Dr. S. Krishnanarayanan currently working as an Assistant Professor in the Department of Computer Science and Engineering at MVJ College Of Engineering, Bangalore, Karnataka, India. He completed his Bachelor of Engineering in Information Technology from the S.Veerasamy College of Engineering and Technology, Puliangudi, Tenkasi, Tamil Nadu, in the year 2009. He completed his Master of Engineering in Computer Science and Engineering from Anand Institute of Higher Technology, Chennai, Tamil Nadu. He has completed PhD in Computer Science and Engineering from Kalasalingam Academy of Research and Education on 2024, Krishnankoil, Tamil Nadu, India. He has 8 years of experience in teaching and 2 years of experience in Industrial.His research areas of interest are Machine Learning, CPS, Information Security.He has already published 6 papers in Scopus Journal and one Book also published.

CONTENT

Chapter I

Chapter II

Chapter III

Chapter IV

Chapter V

Chapter VI

Chapter VII

PREFACE

Artificial Intelligence has become a cornerstone of modern technology, and at its heart lies Deep Learning, a powerful method that enables machines to perceive, learn, and make decisions. From powering virtual assistants to diagnosing diseases and revolutionizing industries, deep learning is no longer a futuristic concept but a transformative reality. Yet, for many, the intricate world of deep learning feels inaccessible, reserved for experts or those with technical expertise. Deep Learning for Everyone is here to change that narrative, offering a clear, concise, and engaging exploration of deep learning that anyone can understand.

This book is crafted to bridge the gap between complexity and comprehension. It introduces you to the foundational ideas of deep learning, explores its practical applications, and discusses its societal implications in a way that is accessible to all readers—whether you're a curious student, a professional seeking to understand AI's impact, or simply an enthusiast eager to learn about the technology shaping our future. By the end of this journey, you'll not only grasp the power of deep learning but also feel inspired to engage with its endless possibilities. Welcome to a world where learning never stops, and innovation knows no bounds!

Authors

1

Getting Started with Deep Learning

In this chapter, we will discuss about some basic concepts of deep learning and their related architectures that will be found in all the subsequent chapters of this book. We'll start with a brief definition of machine learning, whose techniques allow the analysis of large amounts of data to automatically extract information and to make predictions about subsequent new data. Then we'll move onto deep learning, which is a branch of machine learning based on a set of algorithms that attempt to model high-level abstractions in data.

1.1. Introducing machine learning

Machine learning is a computer science research area that deals with methods to identify and implement systems and algorithms by which a computer can learn, based on the examples given in the input. The challenge of machine learning is to allow a computer to learn how to automatically recognize complex patterns and make decisions that are as smart as possible. The entire learning process requires a dataset as follows:

Training set: This is the knowledge base used to train the machine learning algorithm. During this phase, the parameters of the machine learning model (hyperparameters) can be tuned according to the performance obtained.

Testing set: This is used only for evaluating the performance of the model on unseen data.

Learning theory uses mathematical tools that are derived from probability theory of and information theory. This allows you to assess the optimality of some methods over others.

There are basically three learning paradigms that will be briefly discussed:

- ✓ Supervised learning
- ✓ Unsupervised learning
- ✓ Learning with reinforcement

Supervised learning

Supervised learning is the automatic learning task simpler and better known. It is based on a number of preclassified examples, in which, namely, is known a prior the category to which each of the inputs used as examples should belong. In this case, the crucial issue is the problem of generalization. After the analysis of a sample (often small) of examples, the system should produce a model that should work well for all possible inputs.

The set consists of labeled data, that is, objects and their associated classes. This set of labeled examples, therefore, constitutes the training set.

Most of the supervised learning algorithms share one characteristic: the training is performed by the minimization of a particular loss or cost function, representing the output error provided by the system with respect to the desired possible output, because the training set provides us with what must be the desired output.

The system then changes its internal editable parameters, the weights, to minimize this error function. The goodness of the model is evaluated, providing a second set of labeled examples (the test set), evaluating the percentage of correctly classified examples and the percentage of misclassified examples.

The supervised learning context includes the classifiers, but also the learning of functions that predict numeric values. This task is the regression. In a regression problem, the training set is a pair formed by an object and the associated numeric value. There are several supervised learning algorithms that have been developed for classification and regression. These can be grouped into the formula used to represent the classifier or the learned predictor, among all, decision trees, decision rules, neural networks and Bayesian networks.

Unsupervised learning

In unsupervised learning, a set of inputs is supplied to the system during the training phase which, however, contrary to the case supervised learning, is not labeled with the related belonging class. This type of learning is important because in the human brain it is probably far more common than supervised learning.

The only objects in the domain of learning models, in this case, are the observed data inputs, which often is assumed to be independent samples of an unknown underlying probability distribution.

Unsupervised learning algorithms are used particularly used in clustering problems, in which given a collection of objects, we want to be able to understand and show their relationships. A standard approach is to define a similarity measure between two objects, and then look for any cluster of objects that are more similar to each other, compared to the objects in the other clusters.

Reinforcement learning

Reinforcement learning is an artificial intelligence approach that emphasizes the learning of the system through its interactions with the environment. With reinforcement learning, the system adapts its parameters based on feedback received from the environment, which then provides feedback on the decisions made. For example, a system that models a chess player who uses the result of the preceding steps to improve their performance is a system that learns with reinforcement. Current research on learning with reinforcement is highly interdisciplinary, and includes researchers specializing in genetic algorithms, neural networks, psychology, and control engineering.

1.2. What is deep learning

Deep learning is a machine learning research area that is based on a particular type of learning mechanism. It is characterized by the effort to create a learning model at several levels, in which the most profound levels take as input the outputs of previous levels, transforming them and always abstracting more. This insight on the levels of learning is inspired by the way the brain processes information and learns, responding to external stimuli.

Each learning level corresponds, hypothetically, to one of the different areas which make up the cerebral cortex.

1.3. How the human brain works

The visual cortex, which is intended to solve image recognition problems, shows a sequence of sectors placed in a hierarchy. Each of these areas receives an input representation, by means of flow signals that connect it to other sectors.

Each level of this hierarchy represents a different level of abstraction, with the most abstract features defined in terms of those of the lower level. At a time when the brain receives an input image, the processing goes through various phases, for example, detection of the edges or the perception of forms (from those primitive to those gradually more and more complex).

As the brain learns by trial and activates new neurons by learning from the experience, even in deep learning architectures, the extraction stages or layers are changed based on the information received at the input.

The scheme, on the next page shows what has been said in the case of an image classification system, each block gradually extracts the features of the input image, going on to process data already pre-processed from the previous blocks, extracting features of the image that are increasingly abstract, and thus building the hierarchical representation of data that comes with on deep learning based system. More precisely, it builds the layers as follows along with the figure representation:

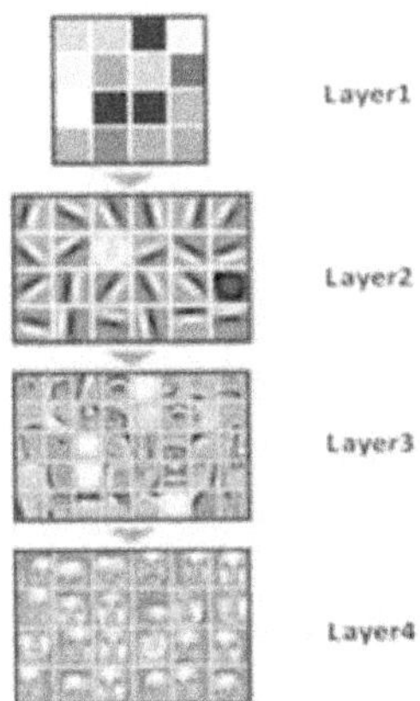

Figure 1.1 a deep learning system at work on a facial classification problem

Layer 1: The system starts identifying the dark and light pixels
Layer 2: The system identifies edges and shapes

Layer 3: The system learns more complex shapes and objects
Layer 4: The system learns which objects define a human face

1.4. Deep learning history

The development of deep learning consequently occurred parallel to the study of artificial intelligence, and especially neural networks. After beginning in the 50 s, it is mainly in the 80s that this area grew, thanks to Geoff Hinton and machine learning specialists who collaborated with him. In those years, computer technology was not sufficiently advanced to allow a real improvement in this direction, so we had to wait until the present day to see, thanks to the availability of data and the computing power, even more significant developments.

1.5. Neural networks

Artificial Neural Networks (ANNs) are one of the main tools that take advantage of the concept of deep learning. They are an abstract representation of our nervous system, which contains a collection of neurons that communicate with each other through connections called axons. The first artificial neuron model was proposed in 1943 by McCulloch and Pitts in terms of a computational model of nervous activity. This model was followed by another, proposed by John von Neumann, Marvin Minsky, Frank Rosenblatt (the so-called perceptron), and many others.

1.6. The biological neuron

As you can see in the following figure, a biological neuron is composed of the following:

- ✓ A cell body or soma
- ✓ One or more dendrites, whose responsibility is to receive signals from other neurons.

- ✓ An axon, which in turn conveys the signals generated by the same neuron to the other connected neurons

This is what a biological neuron model looks like:

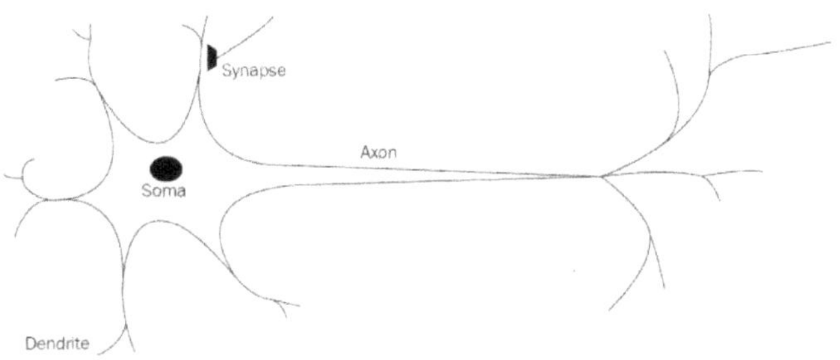

Figure 1.2 Biological neuron model

1.7. An artificial neuron

Similar to the biological one, the artificial neuron consists of the following:

One or more incoming connections, with the task of collecting numerical signals from other neurons; each connection is assigned a weight that will be used to consider each signal sent One or more output connections that carry the signal for the other neurons

An activation function determines the numerical value of the output signal, on the basis of the signals received from the input connections with other neurons, and suitably collected from the weights associated with each picked-up signal and the activation threshold of the neuron itself

The following figure represents the artificial neuron:

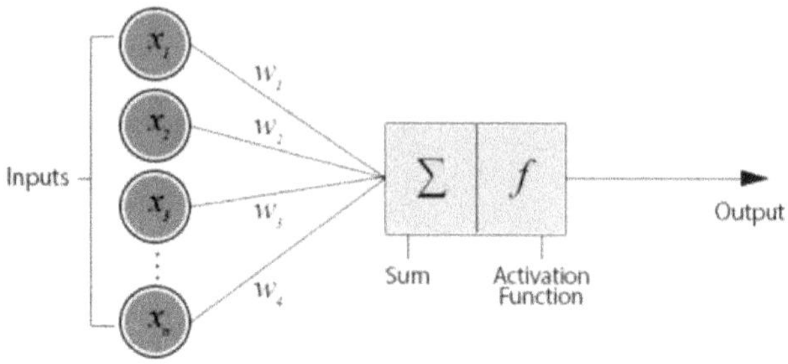

Figure 1.3 neuron model

There is a set of activation functions that differs in complexity and output:

Step function: This fixes the threshold value x (for example, x= 10). The function will return 0 or 1 if the mathematical sum of the inputs is at, above, or below the threshold value.

Linear combination: Instead of managing a threshold value, the weighted sum of the input values is subtracted from a default value; we will have a binary outcome, but it will be expressed by a positive (+b) or negative (-b) output of the subtraction.

Sigmoid: This produces a sigmoid curve, a curve having an S trend. Often, the sigmoid function refers to a special case of the logistic function.From the simplest forms, used in the prototyping of the first artificial neurons, we then move on to more complex ones that allow greater characterization of the functioning of the neuron. The following are just a few:

Hyperbolic tangent function
Radial basis function
Conic section function
Softmax function

It should be recalled that the network, and then the weights in the activation functions, will then be trained. As the selection of the activation function is an important task in the implementation of the network architecture, studies indicate marginal differences in terms of output quality if the training phase is carried out properly.

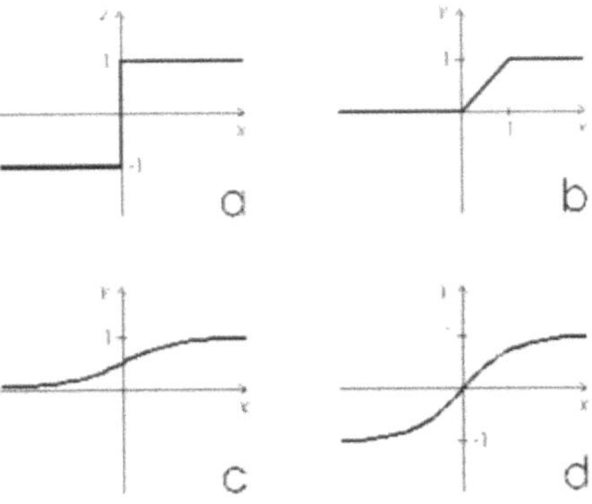

Figure 1.4 most used transfer functions in the preceding figure

1.8. The back propagation algorithm

A supervised learning algorithm used is the back propagation algorithm. The basic steps of the training procedure are as follows:

- ✓ Initialize the net with random weights.
- ✓ For all training cases:
  - o Forward pass: Calculates the error committed by the net, the difference between the desired output and the actual output.
  - o Backward pass: For all layers, starting with the output layer, back to the input layer.
- ✓ Show the network layer output with correct input (error function).

✓ Adapt weights in the current layer to minimize the error function. This is the backpropagation's optimization step. The training process ends when the error on the validation set begins to increase, because this could mark the beginning of a phase of over-fitting of the network, that is, the phase in which the network tends to interpolate the training data at the expense of generalization ability.

1.9. Weights optimization

The availability of efficient algorithms to weights optimization, therefore, constitutes an essential tool for the construction of neural networks. The problem can be solved with an iterative numerical technique called gradient descent (GD).

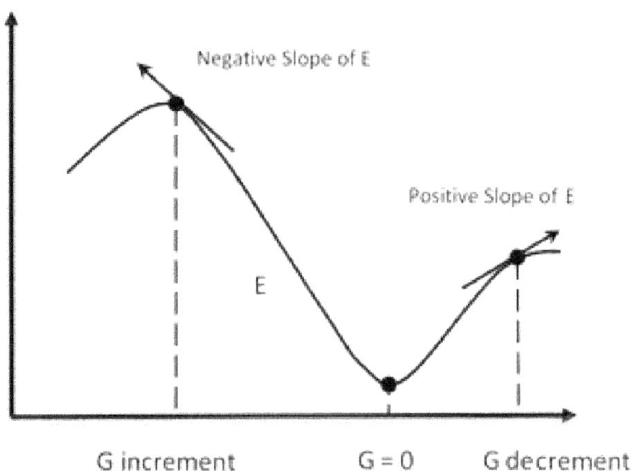

Figure 1.5 Gradient descent procedures

1.10. Stochastic gradient descent

In GD optimization, we compute the cost gradient based on the complete training set; hence, we sometimes also call it batch GD. In the case of very large datasets, using GD can be quite costly, since we are only taking a single step for one pass over the training set. Thus, the larger the training set, the slower our algorithm updates the weights and the longer it may take until it converges to the global cost minimum. An alternative approach and the fastest of gradient descent, and for this reason, used in DNNs, is the Stochastic Gradient Descent (SGD).

In SGD, we use only one training sample from the training set to do the update for a parameter in a particular iteration. Here, the term stochastic comes from the fact that the gradient based on a single training sample is a stochastic approximation of the true cost gradient. Due to its stochastic nature, the path toward the global cost minimum is not direct, as in GD, but may zigzag if we are visualizing the cost surface in a 2D space (see the following figure, (b) Stochastic Gradient Descent - SDG).

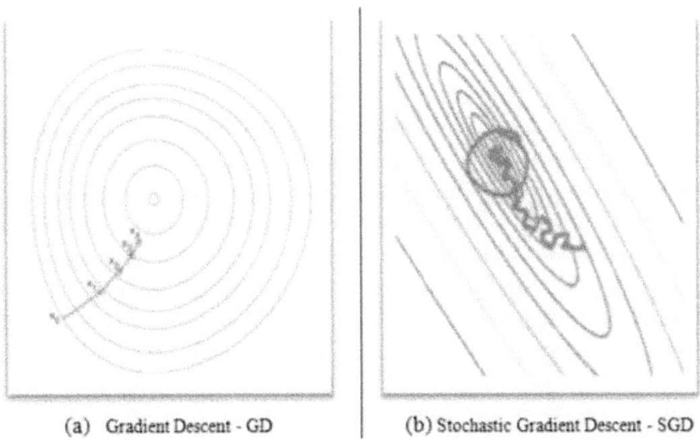

Figure 1.6 GD versus SDG

1.11. Neural network architectures

The way to connect the nodes, the number of layers present, that is, the levels of nodes between input and output, and the number of neurons per layer, defines the architecture of a neural network. There are various types of architecture in neural networks, but this book will focus mainly on two large architectural families.

1.12. Multilayer perception

In multilayer networks, one can identify the artificial neurons of layers such that:

- ✓ Each neuron is connected with all those of the next layer
- ✓ There are no connections between neurons belonging to the same layer There are no connections between neurons belonging to non-adjacent layers
- ✓ The number of layers and of neurons per layer depends on the problem to be solved

Following is the graphical representation of multilayer perception architecture:

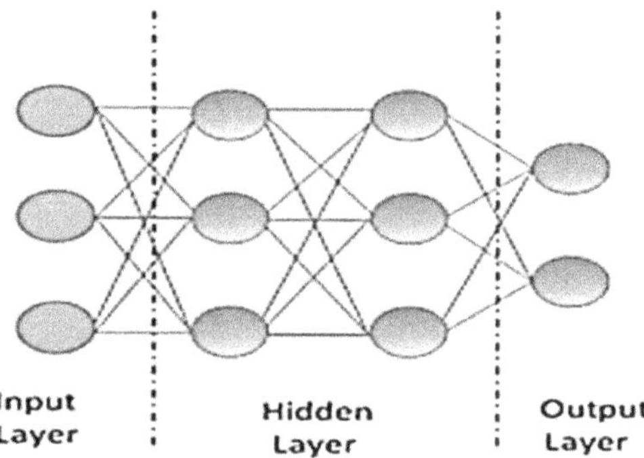

Figure 1.7 multilayer perception architecture

The input and output layers define inputs and outputs; there are hidden layers, whose complexity realizes different behaviours of the network. Finally, the connections between neurons are represented by as many matrices are the pairs of adjacent layers. Each array contains the weights of the connections between the pairs of nodes of two adjacent layers. The feed-forward networks are networks with no loops within the layers.

1.13. DNNs architectures

Deep Neural Networks (DNNs) are artificial neural networks strongly oriented to deep learning. Where normal procedures of analysis are inapplicable due to the complexity of the data to be processed, such networks are an excellent modeling tool. DNNs are neural networks, very similar to those we have discussed, but they must implement a more complex model (a great number of neurons, hidden layers, and connections), although they follow the learning principles that apply to all machine learning problems (that is, supervised learning).

1.14. Convolution Neural Networks

Convolution Neural Networks (CNNs) has been designed specifically for image recognition. Each image used in learning is divided into compact topological portions, each of which will be processed by filters to search for particular patterns. Formally, each image is represented as a three-dimensional matrix of pixels (width, height, and color), and every sub-portion is put on convolution with the filter set. In other words, scrolling each filter along the image computes the inner product of the same filter and input. This procedure produces a set of feature maps (activation maps) for the various filters. By superimposing the various feature maps of the same portion of the image, we get an output volume. This type of layer is called a convolution layer.

The following figure shows a typical CNN architecture:

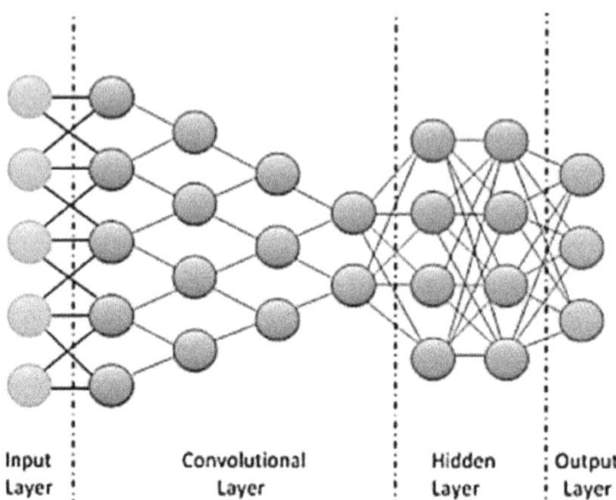

Figure 1.8 Convolution neural network architecture

1.15. Restricted Boltzmann Machines

A Restricted Boltzmann Machine (RBM) consists of a visible and a hidden layer of nodes, but without visible-visible connections and hidden-hidden by the term restricted. These restrictions allow more efficient network training (training that can be supervised or unsupervised).

This type of neural network can represent with few size of the network a large number of features of the inputs; in fact, the n hidden nodes can represent up to 2n features. The network can be trained to respond to a single question (yes/no), up until (again, in binary terms) a total of 2n questions.

The architecture of the RBM is as follows, with neurons arranged according to a symmetrical bipartite graph:

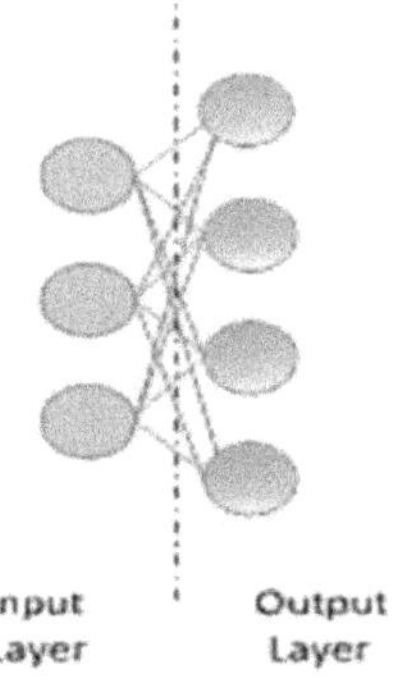

Figure 1.9 Restricted Boltzmann Machine architecture

1.16. Auto encoders

Stacked auto encoders are DNNs that are typically used for data compression. Their particular hourglass structure clearly shows the first part of the process, where the input data is compressed, up to the so-called bottleneck, from which the decompression starts.

The output is then an approximation of the input. These networks are not supervised in the pre training (compression) phase, and the fine-tuning (decompression) phase is supervised:

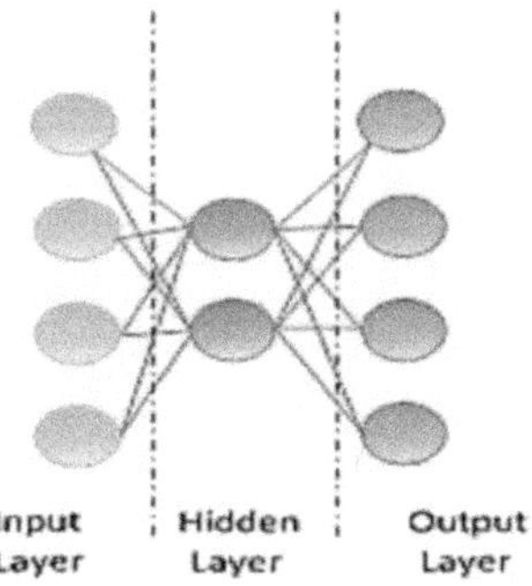

Figure 1.10 Stack auto encoder architecture

1.17. Recurrent Neural Networks

The fundamental feature of a Recurrent Neural Network (RNN) is that the network contains at least one feedback connection, so the activations can flow around in a loop. It enables the networks to do temporal processing and learn sequences, for example, perform sequence recognition/reproduction or temporal association/prediction. RNN architectures can have many different forms. One common type consists of a standard multilayer perceptron (MLP) plus added loops. These can exploit the powerful non-linear mapping capabilities of the MLP, and also have some form of memory. Others have more uniform structures, potentially with every neuron connected to all the others, and may also have stochastic activation functions. For simple architectures and deterministic activation functions, learning can be achieved using similar gradient descent procedures to those leading to the back propagation algorithm for feed-forward networks.

The following figure shows a few of the most important types and features of RNNs:

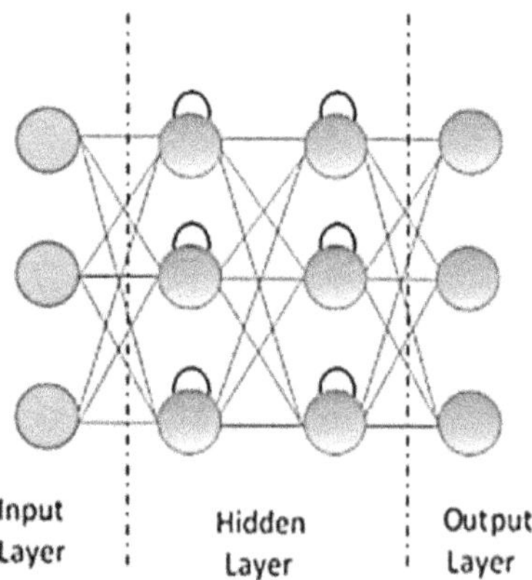

Figure 1.11 Recurrent Neural Network architecture

1.18. Deep learning framework comparisons

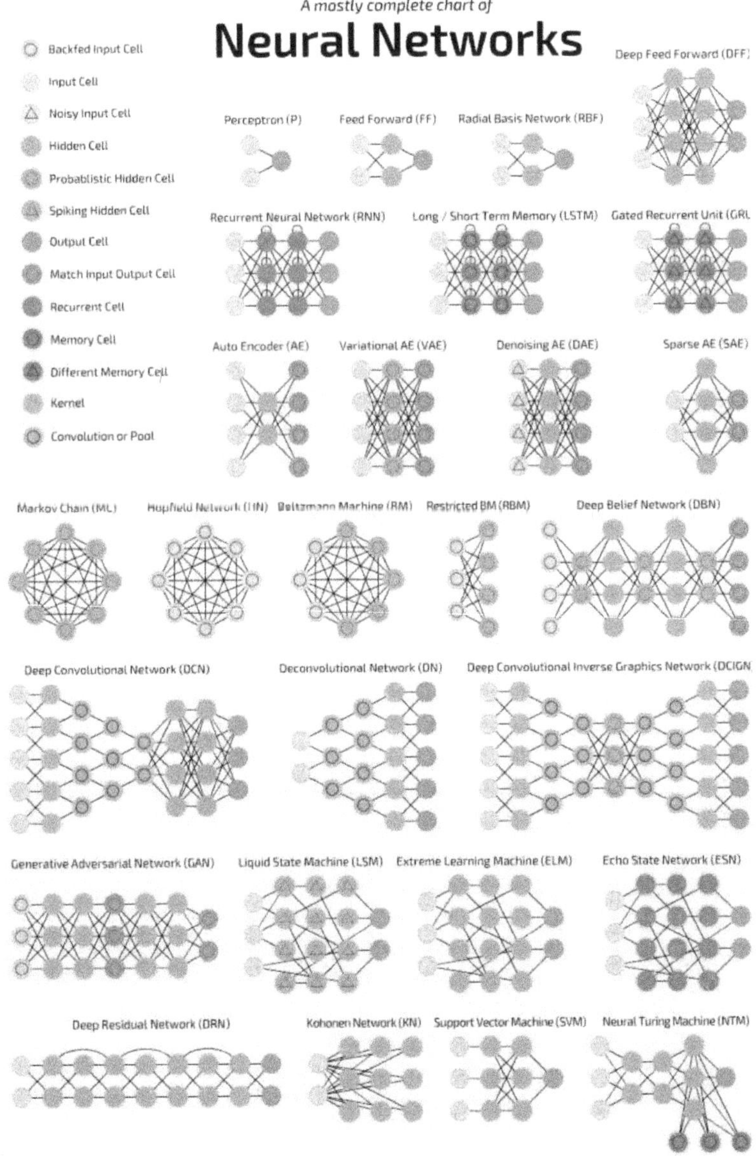

Figure 1.12 complete charts of neural networks (Source: http://www.asimovinstitute.org/neural-network-zoo/)

In short, almost all libraries provide the possibility of using the graphics processor to speed up the learning process, and are released under an open license and are the result of implementation by university research groups.Before starting the comparison, refer figure 13 which is one of the most complete charts of neural networks till date. If you see the URL and related papers, you will find that the idea of neural networks is pretty old and the software frameworks that we are going to compare above also adapts similar architecture during their framework development.

2

Feed-Forward Neural Network

Neural network's architectures can be very different; these configurations are often organized on different layers, the first of which receives the input signals and the last returns the output signals. Usually these networks are identified as feed-forward neural networks.

Feed-forward neural networks, which we intend to illustrate briefly, are well suited to be used for the approximation of functions and for the interpolation.

2.1 Introducing feed-forward neural network

A feed-forward neural network (ffnn) consists of a large number of neurons, organized in layers: one input layer, one or more hidden layers, and one output layer. Each neuron is connected to all the neurons of the previous layer; the connections are not all the same, because they have a different weight. The weights of these connections encode the knowledge of the network.

Data enters at the inputs and passes through the network, layer by layer, until it arrives at the outputs; during this operation there is no feedback between layers. Therefore, these networks are called feed-forward neural networks.

If the neural network architecture is constituted by a low number of hidden layers or neurons, the network is not able to approximate with adequate precision the unknown function, because this is too complex or because the backpropagation algorithm falls within a local minimum. If the network is composed of a high number of hidden layers, we have an over-fitting problem, namely a worsening of the network's generalization ability.

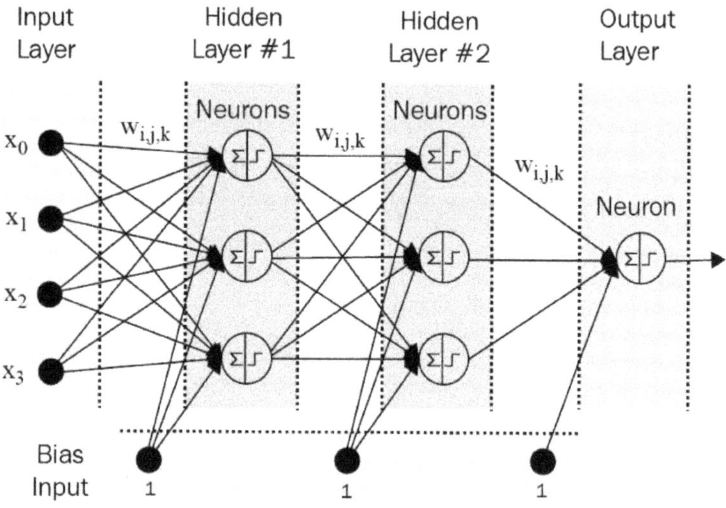

Figure 2.1 feed forward neural network with two hidden layers and an input bias

2.1.1 Feed-forward and back propagation

The back propagation algorithm aims to minimize the error between the current and desired output. Since the network feed-forward, the activation flow always proceeds forward from the input units to the output units. When compared with the output from the one expected, the gradient of the cost function is back propagated through the modification of weights.

This method is recursive and can be applied to any number of hidden layers.

The back propagation algorithm processes the information in such a way that the network decreases the global error during the learning iterations; however, this does not guarantee that the global minimum is reached. The presence of the hidden units and the non-linearity of the output function mean that the behaviour of the error is very complex and has many local minimal. The back propagation algorithm can therefore stop at a local minimum, providing a suboptimal solution. Normally the error always decreases on the training set (that improves the ability to represent the input-output relationship between the data supplied) because the network is learning, while on the testing set (which measures the predictive capabilities), from a certain value then, it can grow due to the over-fitting problem: the resulting network (or model) will have a high classification accuracy for the training samples and a low classification accuracy for unknown samples.

2.1.2 Weights and biases

Besides considering the state of the neuron and the way it is linked to others, we should consider the synaptic weight, which is precisely, the influence of that connection within the network. Each weight has a numerical value indicated by Wij, which is the synaptic weight connecting the neuron i to neuron j.

Depending on the point where a neuron is located, it will always have one or more links, which correspond to relative synaptic weights.

The weights and output function determine the behaviour of an individual neuron and the network in general.

They should be correctly changed during the training phase, to ensure the correct behaviour of the model.

For each unit, i is defined an input vector xi= (x1, x2,...,xn) and a weight vector wi= (wi1, wi2,..., win), and the neuron performs a weighted sum of the inputs:

$$net_i = \sum_j w_{ij} x_j \text{.................. (a)}$$

Among the weights, there is one special, called bias. It is not tied to any other unit of the network and it is considered to have input equal to 1. This expedient allows for establishing a kind of reference point or threshold for neurons, and formally, the bias performs a translation along the abscissa axis to the output function. The previous formula will become as follows:

$$net_i = \sum_j w_{ij} x_j + b_i \text{................................ (b)}$$

2.1.3 Transfer functions

Each neuron receives as input signal the weighted sum of the synaptic weights and the activation values of the neurons connected to it. To allow the neuron to calculate its activation value, that is, what the neuron retransmits, the weighted sum must be passed as the argument of the transfer function. The transfer function allows the receiving neuron to transmit the received signal modifying it.

The domain of this function includes all real numbers and the co-domain is (0, 1). This means that any value will obtain, as output from a neuron per the calculation of its activation state, it will always be between 0 and 1.

The sigmoid function, as represented in the following diagram, provides an interpretation of the saturation rate of a neuron, from not being active (= 0), to its complete saturation, which occurs at a predetermined maximum value (=1):

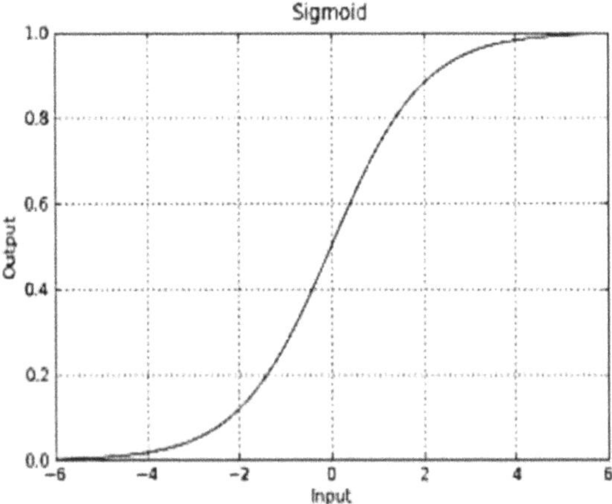

Figure 2.2 Sigmoid function When new data has to be analyzed, it is loaded by the input layer, which through (a) or (b) generates an output.

2.2 Classification of handwritten digits

Automatic recognition of handwritten digits is an important problem, which can be found in many practical applications. In this chapter, we will implement some feed-forward networks to address this problem. To train and test the implemented models we use the MNIST database of handwritten digits. The MNIST dataset is made of a training set of 60,000 examples, plus a test set of 10000 examples. An example of the data, as it is stored in the files of the examples, is shown in the following figure:

Figure 2.3 Example of data extracted from the MNIST database

The source images were originally in black and white, but later, to normalize them to the size of 20 × 20 pixels, intermediate brightness levels have been introduced, due to the effect of the anti-aliasing filter for resizing. Subsequently, the images were focused in the centre of mass of the pixels, in an area of 28×28 pixels, in order to improve the learning process.

2.2.1 Exploring the MNIST dataset

Let's show a short example of how to access the MNIST data and how to display a selected image.

We import the following libraries: The numpy library because we have to do some image manipulation:

>>import numpy as np

The pyplot function in matplotlib for drawing the images:

>>import matplotlib.pyplot as plt

Finally, the mnist_data library, which you can download from the code repository of this book. It is a Google script that allows us to download the MNIST database and to build the dataset:

>>import mnist_data

Then we load the dataset using the read_data_sets method:

```
>>__input = mnist_data.read_data_sets("data")
```

The data is the name of the directory where the images will be uploaded. The shape of the images and labels:

```
>>__input.train.images.shape
(60000, 28, 28, 1)
```

```
>>__input.train.labels.shape
```

(60000, 10)

>>__input.test.images.shape
(10000, 28, 28, 1)

>>__input.test.labels.shape
(10000, 10)

Using the Python library, matplotlib, we want to visualize a single digit: >>image_0 = __input.train.images[0]

>>image_0 = np.resize(image_0,(28,28))

>>label_0 = __input.train.labels[0]
label set = [0. 0. 0. 0. 0. 1. 0. 0. 0. 0.]

The number 1 is the sixth position of the array. It means that the figure for our image is the digit 5.

Finally, we verify that the digit is really 5.

We used the imported plt function, to draw the image_0 tensor:
>>plt.imshow(image_0, cmap='Greys_r')

>>plt.show()

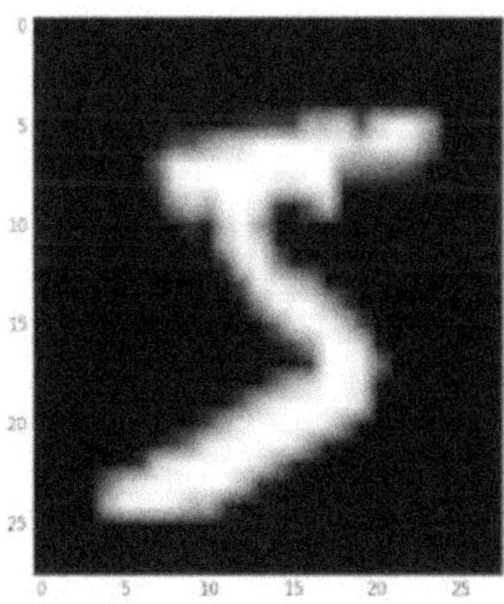

Figure 2.4 The extracted image from the MNIST dataset

2.2.2 Softmax classifier

In the previous section, we showed how to access and manipulate the MNIST dataset. In this section, we will see how to address the classification problem of handwritten digits via the TensorFlow library.

We'll apply the concepts taught to build more models of neural networks in order to assess and compare the results of the different approaches followed. The first feed-forward network architecture that will be implemented is represented in the following figure:

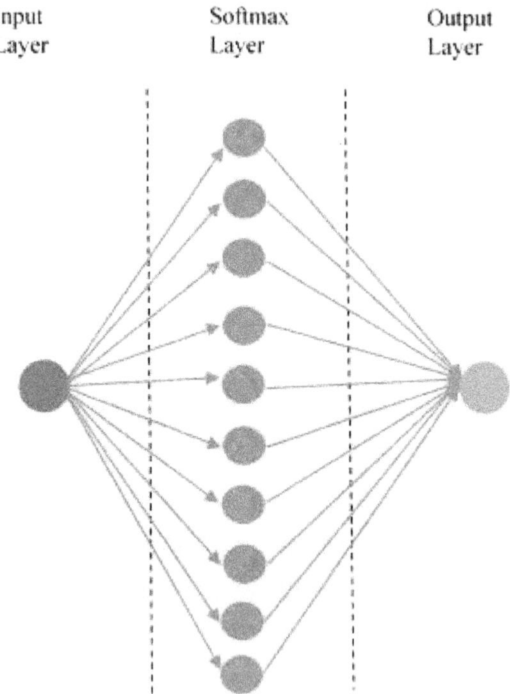

Figure 2.5 The softmax neural network architecture

The hidden layer (or softmax layer) of the network consists of 10 neurons, with a softmax transfer function. Remember that it is defined so that its activation is a set of positive values with total sum equal to 1; this means that the jth value of the output is the probability that j is the class that corresponds with the network input.

Let's see how to implement our neural network model.

The first thing to do is import the necessary libraries and prepare the data for our model:

The first thing to do is import the necessary libraries and prepare the data for our model:

```
import tensorflow as tf
import mnist_data
logs_path = 'log_simple_stats_softmax'
batch_size = 100
learning_rate = 0.5
training_epochs = 10
mnist = mnist_data.read_data_sets("data")
```

Now let's move on to defining the network model.

The input network consists of a set of images extracted from the MNIST datasets; each image has a size of 28x28 pixels:

```
X = tf.placeholder(tf.float32, [None, 28, 28, 1],name="input")
```

The problem is assigning a probability value for each of the possible classes of membership, that is, the digits from 0 to 9. The corresponding output describes a probability distribution from which we can provide a prediction about the value tested. The output network will be contained in the following placeholder, a tensor of 10 elements:

Y_ = tf.placeholder(tf.float32, [None, 10])

The weights take into account the size of the hidden layer (10 neurons) and the input size. The value of the weights must vary at each iteration of the calculation, for which they are defined by the following variable:

W = tf.Variable(tf.zeros([784, 10]))

The matrix weight is W [784, 10] where 784 = 28x28.

Let's flatten the images into a single line of pixels; the number -1 in the shape definition means the only possible dimension that will preserve the number of elements:

XX = tf.reshape(X, [-1, 784])

In a similar way, we define the biases of the network, the effect of which is to control the translatory motion of the trigger relative to the origin of the input signals. Formally, the bias has a role, not different from the weights, which act as an intensity regulator of the emitted/received signals.

The bias tensor is therefore a variable tensor:

b = tf.Variable(tf.zeros([10]))

Also the size (=10) is equal to the total number of neurons of the hidden layer.

The input, weight, and bias tensors are sized to define the evidence parameter that quantifies if a certain image belongs to a particular class:

evidence = tf.matmul(XX, W) + b

The neural network has only one hidden layer, composed of 10 neurons. Using the feed-forward network definition we know that all neurons at the same level must have the same activation function.

In this model, the activation function is the softmax function, it converts the evidence into probabilities of belonging to each of the 10 possible classes:

Y = tf.nn.softmax(evidence,name="output")

The Y output matrix will be formed of 100 rows and 10 columns.

To train our model and to determine if we have a good one, we must define a metric. Indeed, the next goal is to get values for the W and b tensors that minimize the value of a metric and indicate how bad the implemented model is.

Different metrics calculate the degree of error between the desired output and the computed outputs obtained from the training data. The most common error measure is the mean squared error; however, there is some research out there that suggests using other metrics to a neural network like this.

In this example, we use the so-called cross_entropy error function. It is defined as follows:

*cross_entropy = -tf.reduce_mean(Y_ * tf.log(Y)) * 1000.0*

We minimize the error function using the gradient descent algorithm:

train_step = tf.train.GradientDescentOptimizer(0.005).
\minimize(cross_entropy)

Here, we have set the learning rate equal to 0.005.

We will have a correct prediction if the Y network output and the desired output Y_are equal:

```
correct_prediction = tf.equal(tf.argmax(Y, 1),\
tf.argmax(Y_, 1))
```

The correct_prediction variable allows defining the accuracy of the implemented model:

```
accuracy = tf.reduce_mean(tf.cast(correct_prediction,\

tf.float32))
```

We define the summaries that we want to analyze with TensorBoard:

```
tf.summary.scalar("cost", cross_entropy)
tf.summary.scalar("accuracy", accuracy)
summary_op = tf.summary.merge_all()
```

Finally, implemented model is, we must build a session that will take place in the training and testing step:

```
with tf.Session() as sess:
sess.run(tf.global_variables_initializer())
writer = tf.summary.FileWriter(logs_path, \
graph=tf.get_default_graph())
```

The network's training procedure is iterative. It slightly modifies for each learning cycle (or epoch) the synaptic weights by using a selected subset (or batch set): for epoch in range(training_epochs):

It slightly modifies for each learning cycle or epoch the synaptic weights by using a selected set:

batch_count = int(mnist.train.num_examples/batch_size)

The selected sets are respectively batch_x e batch_y:

for i in range(batch_count):

batch_x, batch_y = mnist.train.next_batch(batch_size)

They will be used by the feed_dict statement to feed the network during the training procedure.

At each cycle:

The weights are modified to minimize the error function.

The results are added to the summaries using the following writer.add_summary statement:

```
_, summary = sess.run([train_step, summary_op],\
feed_dict={X: batch_x,\
Y_: batch_y})
writer.add_summary(summary,\
epoch * batch_count + i)
print "Epoch: ", epoch
Finally, we can test the model and evaluate its accuracy:
print "Accuracy: ", accuracy.eval\
(feed_dict={X: mnist.test.images,\
Y_: mnist.test.labels})
print "done"
```

After testing the network, we can, while remaining within the session, run the network model on a single image. For example, we can randomly choose via the randint function, a picture from the mnist.test database:

```
num = randint(0, mnist.test.images.shape[0])
img = mnist.test.images[num]
```

So, we can use the implemented classifier on the selected image:

```
classification = sess.run(tf.argmax(Y, 1), feed_dict={X: [img]})
```

The arguments of the sess.run function are respectively the output and the input of the network. The tf.argmax(Y, 1) function returns the maximum index value for the Y tensor, which is the image we are looking for, the next argument, feed_dict={X: [img]}, allows us to feed the network with the selected image.

Finally, we display the results, that is, the predicted label and the effective label:

```
print 'Neural Network predicted', classification[0]
print 'Real label is:', np.argmax(mnist.test.labels[num])
```

The execution is shown in the following snippet. As you can see, after loading the MNIST data, the training epochs are displayed until the ninth:

```
>>>
Loading data/train-images-idx3-ubyte.mnist
Loading data/train-labels-idx1-ubyte.mnist
Loading data/t10k-images-idx3-ubyte.mnist
Loading data/t10k-labels-idx1-ubyte.mnist
Epoch:     0
Epoch:     1
Epoch:     2
Epoch:     3
Epoch:     4
Epoch:     5
```

Epoch: 6
Epoch: 7
Epoch: 8
Epoch: 9
Then we display the model's accuracy:
Accuracy: 0.9246
done
The predicted and real label:
Neural Network predicted 6
Real label is: 6
>>>

After running the model, we can analyze the execution phases of the executions by using TensorBoard.

2.2.3 Visualization

To run TensorBoard, open the terminal in the folder where the code was executed. Then digit the following command: $> tensorboard --logdir= 'log_simple_stats_softmax'

Once TensorBoard is running, navigate your web browser to localhost:6006 to view the TensorBoard starting page.

When looking at TensorBoard, you will see the navigation tabs in the top right-corner. Each tab represents a set of serialized data that can be visualized.

The following figure shows the computational graph for the implemented classifier:

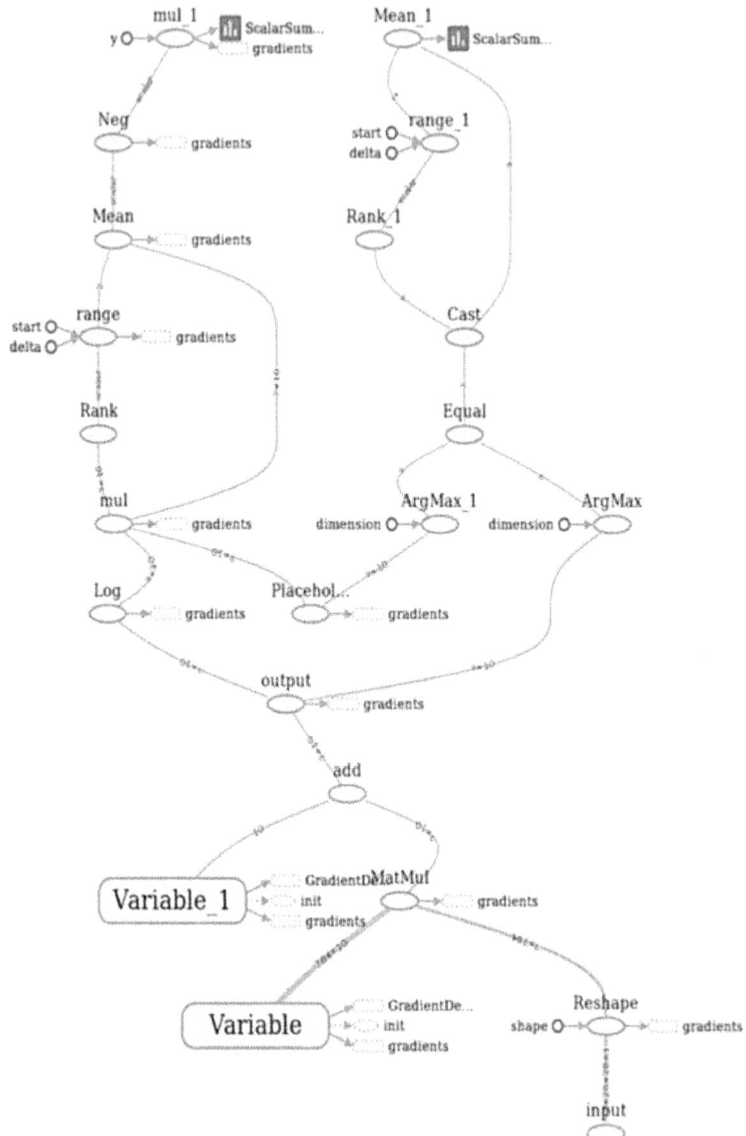

Figure 2.6 Graph representation for the softmax classifier

2.3 How to save and restore a TensorFlow model

Let's suppose we want to use the results of this trained model repeatedly, but without re-training the model each time.

*saver = tf.train.Saver()
save_path = saver.save(sess, "softmax_mnist")*

*
print("Model saved to %s" % save_path)*

2.3.1 Restoring a model

In a second file, we create the following script to restore the deployed network.

Let's start by loading the required libraries:

import matplotlib.pyplot as plt
import tensorflow as tf
import input_data
import numpy as np
import mnist_data
And then by adding the MNIST dataset using the following:
mnist = mnist_data.read_data_sets('data', one_hot=True)
Implement an interactive session:
sess = tf.InteractiveSession()

The following line imports the meta graph saved, which contains all the information we need on the topology of the model and its variables: *new_saver = tf.train.import_meta_graph('softmax_mnist.ckpt.meta')*

Then import the checkpoint file, which contains the weights we developed during training:

new_saver.restore(sess, 'softmax_mnist.ckpt')

To run the loaded model, we need the computation graph, which we call through the following function:

tf.get_default_graph().

The following function will return the default graph being used in the current thread:

tf.get_default_graph().as_graph_def()

We then define the x and y_conv variables and associate them with the nodes that we need to handle in order to feed input and retrieve output: x = sess.graph.get_tensor_by_name("input:0") y_conv = sess.graph.get_tensor_by_name("output:0")

To test the restored model, we take a single image from the MNIST database:

image_b = mnist.test.images[100]

Then we run the restored model, on the selected input:

result = sess.run(y_conv, feed_dict={x:image_b})

The result varaible is the output tensor of 10 items, each of which represents the probability for each digit to be classified. So we print our result and the index with the highest probability, which is just the

classified digit: print(result)
print(sess.run(tf.argmax(result, 1)))

We show the classified image using the plt function imported from matplotlib:

plt.imshow(image_b.reshape([28, 28]), cmap='Greys')
plt.show()

Running the network, we should have the following output:

>>>

Loading data/train-images-idx3-ubyte.mnist
Loading data/train-labels-idx1-ubyte.mnist
Loading data/t10k-images-idx3-ubyte.mnist
Loading data/t10k-labels-idx1-ubyte.mnist

[[5.37428750e-05 6.65060536e-04 1.42298099e-02 3.05720314e-04 2.49665667e-04 6.00658204e-05 9.83844459e-01 4.97680194e-05 4.59994393e-048.17739274e-05]]

The higher array item is 9.83844459e-01 (= 90%), which corresponds to the digit 6, represented as follows:

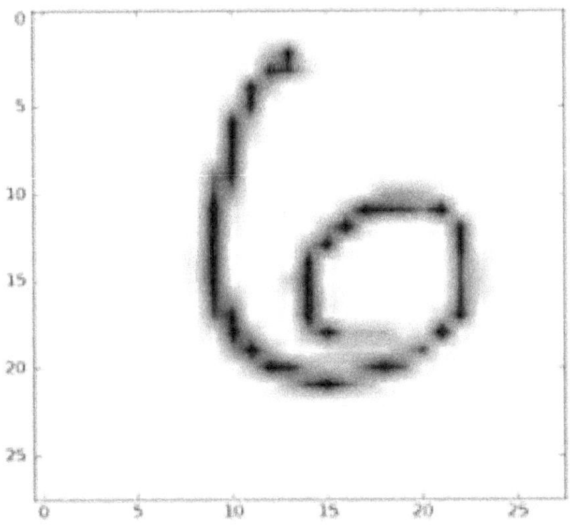

Figure 2.7 Classified image

2.4 Implementing a five-layer neural network

The following implementation increases the network complexity by adding four layers before the softmax layer. To determine the appropriate size of the network, that is, the number of hidden layers and the number of neurons per layer, generally we rely on general empirical criteria, the personal experience, or appropriate tests.

The following table summarizes the implemented network architecture, it shows the number of neurons per layer and the respective activation functions:

Layer	Number of neurons	Activation function
First	L= 200	sigmoid
Second	M=100	sigmoid
Third	N=60	sigmoid
Fourth	O=30	sigmoid
Fifth	10	softmax

The transfer function for the first four layers is the sigmoid function; the last layer of the transfer function is always the softmax since the output of the network must express a probability for the input digit. In general, the number and the size of the intermediate layers greatly affect the network performance:

In a positive way, because on these layers is based the ability of the net to generalize and to detect peculiar characteristics of the input

In a negative way because if the network is redundant it unnecessarily weighs down the learning phase

We will now start to implement the network, importing the following libraries:

```
import mnist_data
import tensorflow as tf
import math
```

Then we will set the following configuration parameters:

```
logs_path = 'log_simple_stats_5_layers_relu_softmax'
batch_size = 100
learning_rate = 0.5
training_epochs = 10
```

We will then download images and labels and prepare the dataset:

```
mnist = mnist_data.read_data_sets("data")
```

Starting with the input layer, we'll now see how to build the network's architecture.

The input layer is now a tensor of the shape [1×784], which represents the image to classify:

```
X = tf.placeholder(tf.float32, [None, 28, 28, 1])
XX = tf.reshape(X, [-1, 784])
```

The first layer receives the pixels of the input image to be classified combined with the W1 weight connections and added to the respective values of the B1 biases tensor:

```
W1 = tf.Variable(tf.truncated_normal([784, L], stddev=0.1))
B1 = tf.Variable(tf.zeros([L]))
```

The first layer sends its output to the second layer, through the sigmoid activation function:

Y1 = tf.nn.sigmoid(tf.matmul(XX, W1) + B1)

The second layer receives the Y1 output from the first layer and combines it with the W2 weight connections and adds it to the respective values of the B2 biases tensor:

W2 = tf.Variable(tf.truncated_normal([L, M], stddev=0.1))
B2 = tf.Variable(tf.zeros([M]))

The second layer sends its output to the third layer, through the sigmoid activation function:

Y2 = tf.nn.sigmoid(tf.matmul(Y1, W2) + B2)

The third layer receives the Y2 output from the second layer and combines it with the W3 weight connections and adds it to the respective values of the B3 biases tensor:

W3 = tf.Variable(tf.truncated_normal([M, N], stddev=0.1))
B3 = tf.Variable(tf.zeros([N]))

The third layer sends its output to the fourth layer, through the sigmoid activation function:

Y3 = tf.nn.sigmoid(tf.matmul(Y2, W3) + B3)

The fourth layer receives the Y3 output from the third layer and combines it with the W4 weight connections and adds it to the respective values of the B4 biases tensor:

W4 = tf.Variable(tf.truncated_normal([N, O], stddev=0.1))
B4 = tf.Variable(tf.zeros([O]))

It sends its output to the fifth layer, through the sigmoid activation function:

Y4 = tf.nn.sigmoid(tf.matmul(Y3, W4) + B4)

The fifth layer will receive in input the O = 30 stimuli coming from the fourth layer that will be converted in the respective classes of probability for each number, through the softmax activation function:

W5 = tf.Variable(tf.truncated_normal([O, 10], stddev=0.1))
B5 = tf.Variable(tf.zeros([10]))
Ylogits = tf.matmul(Y4, W5) + B5
Y = tf.nn.softmax(Ylogits)

Here, our loss function is the cross-entropy between the target and the softmax activation function applied to the model's prediction:

cross_entropy = tf.nn.softmax_cross_entropy_with_logits (logits=Ylogits, labels=Y_)cross_entropy = tf.reduce_mean(cro

The tf.train.AdamOptimizer uses the Kingma and Ba's Adam algorithm (https://arxiv.org/pdf/1412.6980v8.pdf) to control the learning rate. AdamOptimizer offers several advantages over the simple tf.train.GradientDescentOptimizer; in fact, it uses a larger effective step size, and the algorithm will converge to this step size without fine tuning:

learning_rate = 0.003 train_step = tf.train.AdamOptimizer (learning_rate).minimize (cross_entropy)

Also, we define the correct_prediction and the model's accuracy:

correct_prediction = tf.equal(tf.argmax(Y, 1), tf.argmax(Y_, 1)) accuracy = tf.reduce_mean(tf.cast(correct_prediction, tf.float32))

The source code for the definition of the summaries and the running of the session is almost identical to the previous. We can pass directly to evaluate the implemented model. Running the model, we have the following output. The final test set accuracy after running this code should be approximately 97%:

```
>>>
Loading data/train-images-idx3-ubyte.mnist
Loading data/train-labels-idx1-ubyte.mnist
Loading data/t10k-images-idx3-ubyte.mnist
Loading data/t10k-labels-idx1-ubyte.mnist
Epoch:0
Epoch:1
Epoch:2
Epoch:3
Epoch:4
Epoch:5
Epoch:6
Epoch:7
Epoch:8
Epoch:9
Accuracy:0.9744
done
>>>
```

Visualization

We can now move onto TensorBoard, by simply opening the terminal in the running folder, followed by this command:

$> Tensorboard --logdir = 'log_simple_stats_5_layers_relu_softmax'

Then open your browser at localhost .

In the following figure, we show the trend of the cost function as a function of the number of examples

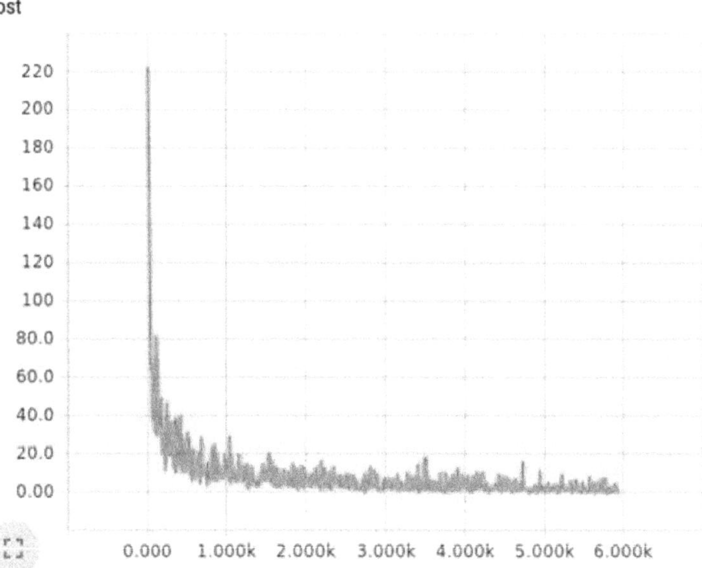

Figure 2.8 Cost function over train set

The cost function decreases with increasing iterations. This pattern is correct; it is exactly shown in the preceding figure. If this doesn't happen, it means that something went wrong: in the best case, it could simply be due to the fact that some parameters have not been set properly; at worst, it could be a problem in the constructed dataset, for example, too little information, poor quality images, or more. In this case, we must directly fix the dataset.

2.5 Dropout optimization

During the learning phase, the connections with the next layer can be limited to a subset of neurons to reduce the weights to be updated, this learning optimization technique is called dropout. The dropout is therefore a technique used to decrease the overfitting within a network with many layers and/or neurons. In general, the dropout layers are positioned after the layers that possess a large amount of trainable neurons.

This technique allows setting to 0, and then excluding the activation of a certain percentage of the neurons of the preceding layer. The probability that the neuron's activation is set to 0 is indicated by the dropout ratio parameter within the layer, via a number between 0 and 1: in practice the activation of a neuron is held with probability equal to the dropout ratio, otherwise it is discarded, that is, set to 0.

The neurons by this transaction do not affect, therefore, during the forward propagation and even during the next backward propagation of a certain input. In this way, for each input, the network owns an architecture slightly different from the previous, some connections are active and some are not, in a different way, every time, even if these architectures possess the same weights. The following figure shows how the dropout works: each hidden unit is randomly omitted from the network with a probability of p. One thing to notice though, is that the selected dropout units are different for each training instance, that's why this is more of a training problem, rather dropout can be seen as an efficient way to perform model averaging across a large number of different neural networks, where overfitting can be avoided with much less cost of computation than an architecture problem:

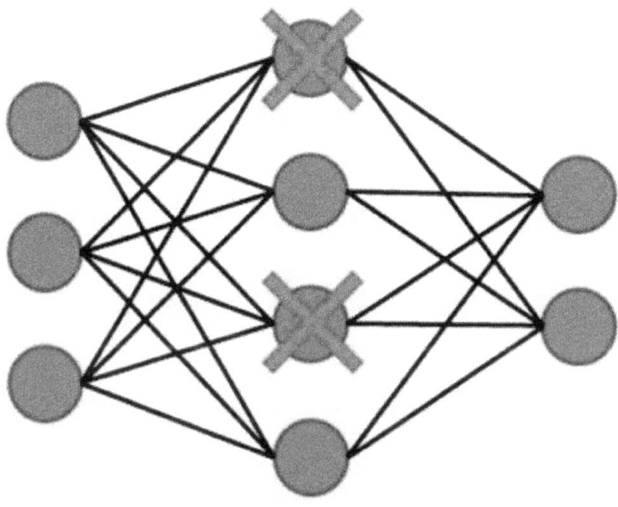

Figure 2.9 Dropout representation

The dropout reduces the possibility that a neuron relies on the presence of other neurons, in this way it is forced to learn more about robust features and that they are also useful with linkages to other different neurons.

The TensorFlow function that allows building a dropout layer is tf.nn.dropout.

The input of this function is the output of the previous layer and a dropout parameter; tf.nn.dropout, returns an output tensor of the same size of the input tensor.

The implementation of this model follows the same rules used for the 5-layer network; in this case, between one layer and another layer we must insert the dropout function:

```
dropout_ratio = tf.placeholder(tf.float32)
Y1 = tf.nn.relu(tf.matmul(XX, W1) + B1)
Y1d = tf.nn.dropout(Y1, dropout_ratio)
```

```
Y2 = tf.nn.relu(tf.matmul(Y1d, W2) + B2)
Y2d = tf.nn.dropout(Y2, dropout_ratio)
Y3 = tf.nn.relu(tf.matmul(Y2d, W3) + B3)
Y3d = tf.nn.dropout(Y3, dropout_ratio)
Y4 = tf.nn.relu(tf.matmul(Y3d, W4) + B4)
Y4d = tf.nn.dropout(Y4, dropout_ratio)
Ylogits = tf.matmul(Y4d, W5) + B5
Y = tf.nn.softmax(Ylogits)
```

The dropout optimization produces the following results:

```
>>>
Loading data/train-images-idx3-ubyte.mnist
Loading data/train-labels-idx1-ubyte.mnist
Loading data/t10k-images-idx3-ubyte.mnist
Loading data/t10k-labels-idx1-ubyte.mnist
Epoch:0
Epoch:1
Epoch:2
Epoch:3
Epoch:4
Epoch:5
Epoch:6
Epoch:7
Epoch:8
Epoch:9
Accuracy:0.9666
done
>>>
```

Visualization

To start the TensorBoard analysis, just type the following: *$> Tensorboard --logdir = 'log_simple_stats_5_lyers_dropout'*

The following graph shows the accuracy cost function as a function of the training examples:

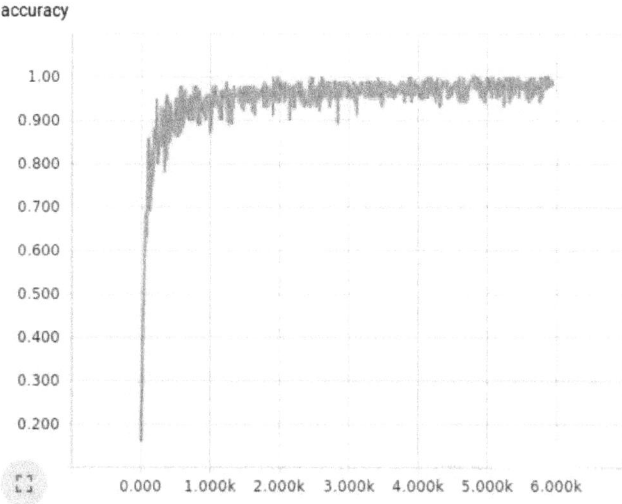

Figure 2.10 Accuracy in dropout optimization

In the following chart, we display the cost function as a function of the training examples:

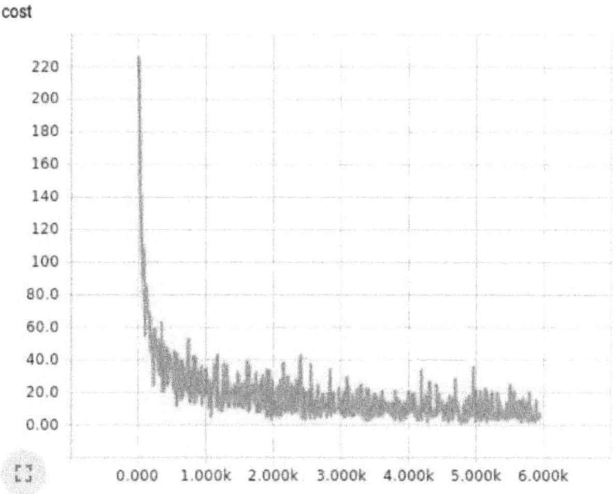

Figure 2.11 The cost function over the training set

3

Convolutional Neural Network

Convolutional Neural Networks (CNNs) are deep learning networks, which have achieved excellent results in many practical applications, and primarily in object recognition of images. CNN architecture is organized into a series of blocks. The first blocks are composed of two types of layers, convolutional layers and pooling layers; while the last blocks are fully-connected layers with softmax layers.

We'll develop two examples of CNN networks, for image classification problems. The first problem is the classic MNIST digit classification system. We'll see how to build a CNN that reaches 99 percent accuracy. The training set for the second example is taken from the Kaggle platform. The purpose here is to train a network on a series of facial images to classify their emotional stretch.

We'll evaluate the accuracy of the model and then we'll test it on a single image that does not belong to the original dataset.

3.1 Introducing CNN networks

In recent years, Deep Neural Networks (DNNs) have contributed a new impetus to research as well as industry and are therefore been used increasingly. A special type of a DNN is a Convolutional Neural Network (CNN), which has been used with great success in image classification problems.

Before diving into the implementation of an image classifier based on CNN, we'll introduce some basic concepts in image recognition, such as feature detection and convolution.

It's well known that a real image is associated with a grid composed of a high number of small squares, called pixels. The following figure represents a black and white image related to a 5x5 grid of pixels:

Figure 3.1 Black and white image

Each element of the grid corresponds to a pixel and, in the case of a black and white image, it assumes either a value of 1, which is associated with black color or the value 0, which is associated with white image. In a grayscale image, the values for each grid element are in the range [0-255], where 0 is associated with black and 255 with white.

Finally, a color image is represented by a group of three matrices, each corresponding to one color channel (red, green, blue); and each element of each matrix can vary over an entire interval [0.255] that specifies the brightness of the fundamental color (or base color).

This representation is shown in the following figure where each represented matrix is a 4x4 size and the number of color channels is three:

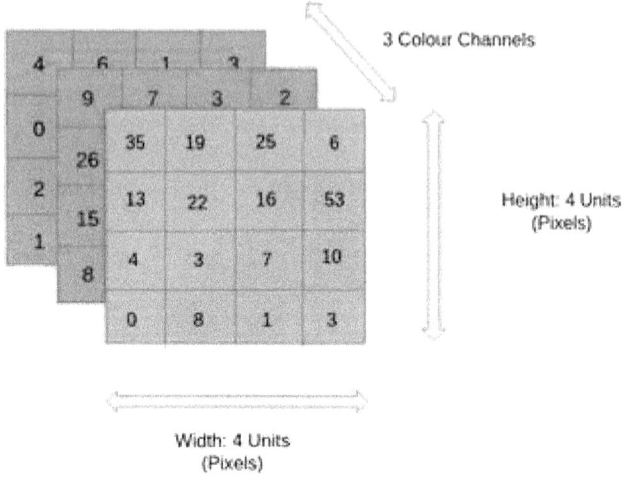

Figure 3.2 Color image representation

Let's focus now on the black and white image (5x5 matrix), and suppose to flow on this matrix, top to bottom and from left to right, a second matrix of lower dimensions, for example a 3x3 matrix, as shown in the following figure:

$$\begin{bmatrix} 1 & 0 & 1 \\ 0 & 1 & 0 \\ 1 & 0 & 1 \end{bmatrix}$$

Figure 3.3 Kernel filter

This flowing matrix is called a kernel filter or feature detector. While the kernel filter moves along the input matrix (or input image), it performs a scalar product, between the kernel values and those of the matrix portion to which it is applied. The result is a new matrix, called a convolution matrix.

The following figure points out the convolution procedure, the convolved feature (the resulting 3x3 matrix) is generated by the convolution operation, flowing the kernel filter (the 3x3 matrix) on the input image (the 5x5 matrix):

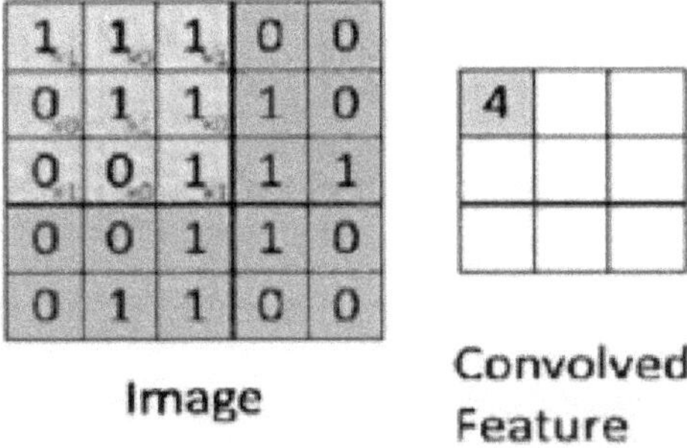

Figure 3.4 Input image, kernel filter and convolved feature

3.2 CNN architecture

CNN architecture

Taking as an example the input matrix 5x5 as shown earlier, a CNN consists of an input layer consisting of 25 neurons (5x5 = 25) whose task is to acquire the input value corresponding to each pixel and transfer it to the next hidden layer.

In a multilayer network, the outputs of all neurons of the input layer would be connected to each neuron of the hidden layer (fully-connected layer).

In CNN networks, the connection scheme that defines the convolutional layer that we are going to describe is significantly different.

As you can probably guess, this is the main type of layer; the use of one or more of these layers in a CNN is indispensable.

In a convolutional layer, each neuron is connected to a certain region of the input area called the receptive field.

For example, using a 3x3 kernel filter, each neuron will have a bias and 9=3x3 weights connected to a single receptive field. Of course, to effectively recognize an image, we need different kernel filters applied to the same receptive field, because each filter should recognize a different feature's image.

The set of neurons that identify the same feature define a single feature map.

The following figure shows a CNN architecture in action; the input image of a size of 28x28 will be analyzed by a convolutional layer composed of a 32 features map with a size of 28x28. The figure also shows a receptive field and the kernel filter of a 3x3 size:

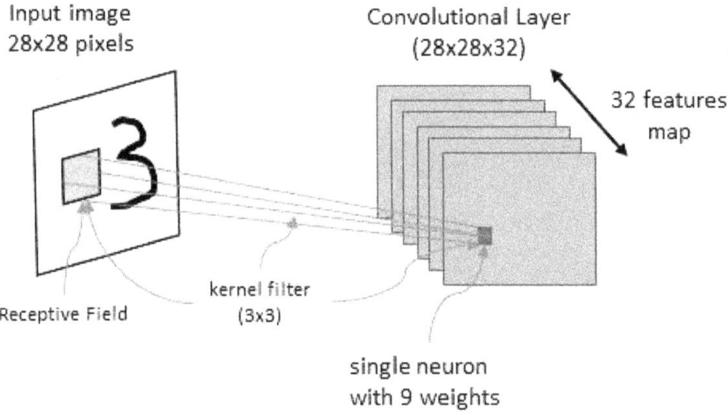

Figure 3.5 CNN in action

A CNN may consist of several convolution layers connected in a cascade. The output of each convolution layer is a set of feature maps (each generated by a single kernel filter), and all these matrices define a new input that will be used by the next layer.

3.3 A model for CNNs – LeNet

Convolutional and max-pooling layers are at the heart of the LeNet family models. It is a family of multilayered feed-forward networks specialized on visual pattern recognition.

While the exact details of the model will vary greatly, the following figure points out the graphical schema of a LeNet network:

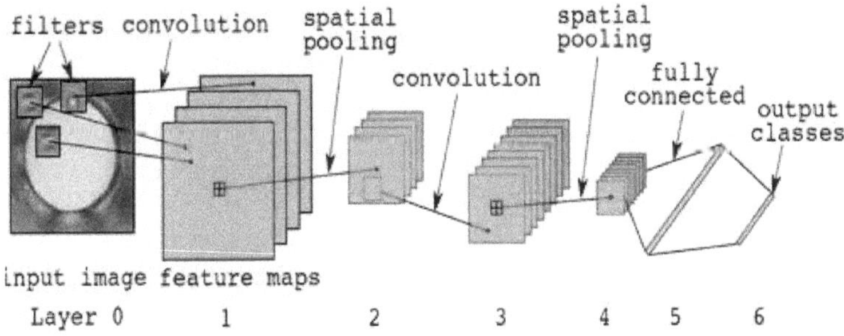

Figure 3.6 CNN in action

In a LeNet model, the lower layers are composed of an alternating convolution and max-pooling, while the last layers are fully-connected and correspond to a traditional feed-forward network (fully-connected + softmax layer).

The input to the first fully-connected layer is the set of all feature maps at the layer below.

From a TensorFlow implementation point of view, this means lower layers operate on 4D tensors. These are then flattened to a 2D matrix to be compatible with a feed forward implementation.

3.4 Building your first CNN

In this section, we will learn how to build a CNN to classify images of the MNIST dataset. In the previous chapter, we saw that a simple softmax model provides about 92% classification accuracy for recognizing hand written digits in the MNIST.

Here we'll implement a CNN which has a classification accuracy of about 99%.

The following figure shows how the data flows in the first two convolutional layer. The input image is processed in the first convolutional layer using the filter-weights. This results in 32 new images, one for each filter in the convolutional layer. The images are also downsampled with the pooling operation so the image resolution is decreased from 28x28 to 14x14.

These 32 smaller images are then processed in the second convolutional layer. We need filter weights again for each of these 32 features, and we need filter-weights for each output channel of this layer. The images are again downsampled with a pooling operation so that the image resolution is decreased from 14x14 to 7x7. The total number of features for this convolutional layer is 64:

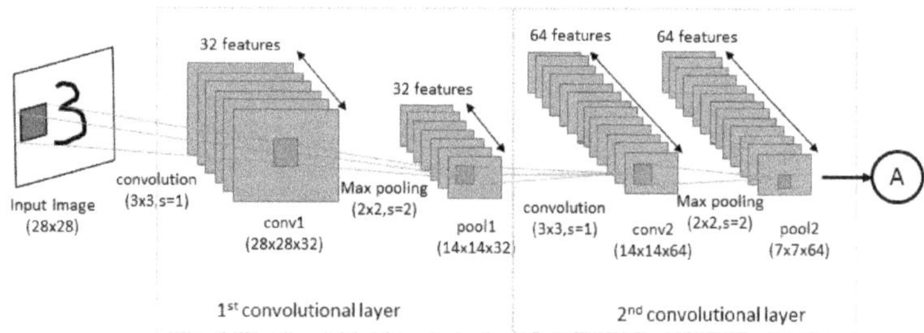

Figure 3.7 Data flow of the first two convolutional layers

The 64 resulting images are filtered again by a (3×3) third convolutional layer. We don't apply a pooling operation for this layer. The output of the second convolutional layer is 128 images of 7×7 pixels each. These are then flattened to a single vector of length 4×4×128, which is used as the input to a fully-connected layer with 128 neurons (or elements).

This feeds into another fully-connected layer with 10 neurons, one for each of the classes, which is used to determine the class of the image, that is, which number is depicted in the following image:

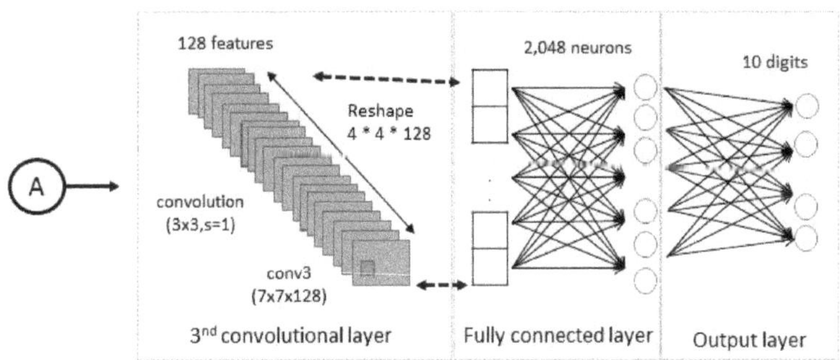

Figure 3.8 Data flow of the last three convolutional layers

The convolutional filters are initially chosen at random. The error between the predicted and actual class of the input image is measured as the so-called cost function which generalizes our network beyond the training data. The optimizer then automatically propagates this error back through the convolutional network and updates the filter-weights to improve the classification error.

This is done iteratively thousands of times until the classification error is sufficiently low.

Now let's see in detail how to code our first CNN.

Let's start by importing the TensorFlow libraries for our implementation:

import tensorflow as tf
import numpy as np
from tensorflow.examples.tutorials.mnist import input_data

Set the following parameters, that indicate the number of samples to consider respectively for the training phase (128) and then the test phase (256):

batch_size = 128
test_size = 256

We define the following parameter, the value is 28 because a MNIST image is 28 pixels in height and width:

img_size = 28

Regarding the number of classes, the value 10 means that we'll have one class for each of 10 digits:

num_classes = 10

A placeholder variable, X, is defined for the input images. The data type for this tensor is set to float32 and the shape is set to [None, img_size, img_size, 1], where None means that the tensor may hold an arbitrary number of images:

X = tf.placeholder("float", [None, img_size, img_size, 1])

Then we set another placeholder variable, Y, for the true labels associated with the images that were input data in the placeholder variable X.

The shape of this placeholder variable is [None, num_classes] which means it may hold an arbitrary number of labels and each label is a vector of the length num_classes which is 10 in this case:

Y = tf.placeholder("float", [None, num_classes])

We collect the mnist data which will be copied into the data folder:

mnist = mnist_data.read_data_sets("data/")

We build the datasets for training (trX, trY) and testing the network (teX, teY):

```
trX, trY, teX, teY = mnist.train.images,\
mnist.train.labels,\
mnist.test.images,\
mnist.test.labels
```

The trX and teX image sets must be reshaped according the input shape:

```
trX = trX.reshape(-1, img_size, img_size, 1)
teX = teX.reshape(-1, img_size, img_size, 1)
```

We shall now proceed to define the network's weights.

The init_weights function builds new variables in the given shape and initializes the network's weights with random values:

```
def init_weights(shape):
return tf.Variable(tf.random_normal(shape, stddev=0.01))
```

Each neuron of the first convolutional layer is convoluted to a small subset of the input tensor, with a dimension of 3x3x1, while the value 32 is just the number of feature maps we are considering for this first layer. The weight w is then defined:

```
w = init_weights([3, 3, 1, 32])
```

The number of inputs is then increased of 32, which means that each neuron of the second convolutional layer is convoluted to 3x3x32 neurons of the first convolution layer. The w2 weight is:

```
w2 = init_weights([3, 3, 32, 64])
```

The value 64 represents the number of obtained output features.

The third convolutional layer is convoluted to 3x3x64 neurons of the previous layer, while 128 are the resulting features:

```
w3 = init_weights([3, 3, 64, 128])
```

The fourth layer is fully-connected. It receives 128x4x4 inputs, while the output is equal to 625:

```
w4 = init_weights([128 * 4 * 4, 625])
```

The output layer receives 625 inputs, while the output is the number of classes:

```
w_o = init_weights([625, num_classes])
```

TensorFlow graph:

```
p_keep_conv = tf.placeholder("float")
p_keep_hidden = tf.placeholder("float")
```

It's time to define the network model. As we did for the network's weight definition, it will be a function.

It receives as input, the X tensor, the weights tensors, and the dropout parameters for convolution and fully-connected layers:

def model(X, w, w2, w3, w4, w_o, p_keep_conv, p_keep_hidden):

The tf.nn.conv2d() function executes the TensorFlow operation for the convolution. Note that the strides are set to 1 in all dimensions.

Indeed, the first and last stride must always be 1, because the first is for the image number and the last is for the input channel. The padding parameter is set to 'SAME' which means the input image is padded with zeroes so that the size of the output is the same:

conv1 = tf.nn.conv2d(X, w,strides=[1, 1, 1, 1],padding='SAME')

Then we pass the conv1 layer to a relu layer. It calculates the max(x, 0) function for each input pixel x, adding some non-linearity to the formula and allows us to learn more complicated functions:

conv1 = tf.nn.relu(conv1)

The resulting layer is then pooled by the tf.nn.max_pool operator:

conv1 = tf.nn.max_pool(conv1, ksize=[1, 2, 2, 1]
,strides=[1, 2, 2, 1],
padding='SAME')

It is a 2x2 max-pooling, which means that we are considering 2x2 windows and select the largest value in each window. Then we move two pixels to the next window.

We try to reduce the overfitting, via the tf.nn.dropout() function, passing the conv1 layer and the p_keep_conv probability value:

```
conv1 = tf.nn.dropout(conv1, p_keep_conv)
```

As you can see, the next two convolutional layers, conv2, conv3, are defined in the same way as conv1:

```
conv2 = tf.nn.conv2d(conv1, w2,
strides=[1, 1, 1, 1],
padding='SAME')
conv2 = tf.nn.relu(conv2)
conv2 = tf.nn.max_pool(conv2, ksize=[1, 2, 2, 1],
strides=[1, 2, 2, 1],
padding='SAME')
conv2 = tf.nn.dropout(conv2, p_keep_conv)
conv3=tf.nn.conv2d(conv2, w3,
strides=[1, 1, 1, 1]
,padding='SAME')
conv3_a = tf.nn.relu(conv3)
```

Two fully-connected layers are added to the network. The input of the first FC_layer is the convolution layer from the previous convolution:

```
FC_layer = tf.nn.max_pool(conv3, ksize=[1, 2, 2, 1],
strides=[1, 2, 2, 1],
padding='SAME')
FC_layer = tf.reshape(FC_layer, [-
1,w4.get_shape().as_list()[0]])
```

A dropout function is again used to reduce the overfitting:

```
FC_layer = tf.nn.dropout(FC_layer, p_keep_conv)
```

The output layer receives the input as FC_layer and the w4 weight tensor. A relu and a dropout operator are respectively applied:

```
output_layer = tf.nn.relu(tf.matmul(FC_layer, w4))
output_layer = tf.nn.dropout(output_layer, p_keep_hidden)
```

The result variable is a vector of length 10 for determining which one of the 10 classes for the input image belongs to:

```
result = tf.matmul(output_layer, w_o)
return result
```

The cross-entropy is the performance measure we used in this classifier. The cross-entropy is a continuous function that is always positive and is equal to zero, if the predicted output exactly matches the desired output. The goal of this optimization is therefore to minimize the cross-entropy so it gets as close to zero as possible by changing the variables of the network layers.

TensorFlow has a built-in function for calculating the cross-entropy. Note that the function calculates the softmax internally so we must use the output of py_x directly:

```
py_x = model(X, w, w2, w3, w4, w_o, p_keep_conv,
p_keep_hidden)
```

```
Y_ = tf.nn.softmax_cross_entropy_with_logits(logits=py_x,
labels=Y)
```

Now that we have defined the cross-entropy for each classified image, we have a measure of how well the model performs on each image individually. But using the cross-entropy to guide the optimization of the networks's variables we need a single scalar value, so we simply take the average of the cross-entropy for all the classified images:

cost = tf.reduce_mean(Y_)

To minimize the evaluated cost, we must define an optimizer. In this case, we adopt the implemented RMSPropOptimizer function which is an advanced form of gradient descent.

The RMSPropOptimizer function implements the RMSProp algorithm, that is an unpublished, adaptive learning rate method proposed by Geoff Hinton in Lecture 6e of his coursera class.

The RMSPropOptimizer function also divides the learning rate by an exponentially decaying average of squared gradients. Hinton suggests setting the decay parameter to 0.9, while a good default value for the learning rate is 0.001:

optimizer = tf.train.RMSPropOptimizer(0.001, 0.9).minimize(cost)

Basically, the common Stochastic Gradient Descent (SGD) algorithm has a problem in that learning rates must scale with 1/T to get convergence, where T is the iteration number. RMSProp tries to get around this by automatically adjusting the step size so that the step is on the same scale as the gradients, as the average gradient gets smaller, the coefficient in the SGD update gets bigger to compensate.

Finally, we define predict_op that is the index with the largest value across dimensions from the output of the mode:

predict_op = tf.argmax(py_x, 1)

Note that optimization is not performed at this point. Nothing is calculated at all; we'll just add the optimizer object to the TensorFlow graph for later execution.

We now come to define the network's running session: There are 55,000 images in the training set, so it takes a long time to calculate the gradient of the model using all these images. Therefore, we'll use a small batch of images in each iteration of the optimizer. If your computer crashes or becomes very slow because you run out of RAM, then you can try and lower this number, but you may then need to perform more optimization iterations.

Now we can proceed to implement a TensorFlow session:

with tf.Session() as sess:
sess.run(tf.global_variables_initializer())
for i in range(100):

We get a batch of training examples, the training_batch tensor now holds a subset of images and corresponding labels:

training_batch =zip(range(0, len(trX), batch_size),
range(batch_size,
len(trX)+1,
batch_size))

Put the batch into feed_dict with the proper names for placeholder variables in the graph. We run the optimizer using this batch of training data, TensorFlow assigns the variables in a feed to the placeholder variables and then runs the optimizer:

for start, end in training_batch:

sess.run(optimizer, feed_dict={X: trX[start:end],

Y: trY[start:end], p_keep_conv: 0.8, p_keep_hidden: 0.5})

At the same time, we get a shuffled batch of test samples:

```
test_indices = np.arange(len(teX))
np.random.shuffle(test_indices)
test_indices = test_indices[0:test_size]
```

For each iteration, we display the accuracy evaluated on the batch set:

```
print(i, np.mean(np.argmax(teY[test_indices], axis=1) ==
sess.run
(predict_op, feed_dict={X: teX[test_indices],
Y: teY[test_indices], p_keep_conv: 1.0, p_keep_hidden: 1.0})))
```

Training a network can take several hours depending on how much computational resources it uses. The results on my machine are as follows:

```
Successfully downloaded train-images-idx3-ubyte.gz 9912422 bytes.
Successfully extracted to train-images-idx3-ubyte.mnist 9912422 bytes.
Loading ata/train-images-idx3-ubyte.mnist
Successfully downloaded train-labels-idx1-ubyte.gz 28881 bytes.
Successfully extracted to train-labels-idx1-ubyte.mnist 28881 bytes.
Loading ata/train-labels-idx1-ubyte.mnist
Successfully downloaded t10k-images-idx3-ubyte.gz 1648877 bytes.
Successfully extracted to t10k-images-idx3-ubyte.mnist 1648877 bytes.
Loading ata/t10k-images-idx3-ubyte.mnist
Successfully downloaded t10k-labels-idx1-ubyte.gz 4542 bytes.
Successfully extracted to t10k-labels-idx1-ubyte.mnist 4542 bytes.
Loading ata/t10k-labels-idx1-ubyte.mnist
(0, 0.95703125)
(1, 0.98046875)
(2, 0.9921875)
```

(3, 0.99609375)
(4, 0.99609375)
(5, 0.98828125)
(6, 0.99609375)
(7, 0.99609375)
(8, 0.98828125)
(9, 0.98046875)
(10, 0.99609375)
(90, 1.0)
(91, 0.9921875)
(92, 0.9921875)
(93, 0.99609375)
(94, 1.0)
(95, 0.98828125)
(96, 0.98828125)
(97, 0.99609375)
(98, 1.0)
(99, 0.99609375)

3.5 Emotion recognition with CNNs

One of the hardest problems to solve in deep learning has nothing to do with neural nets, it's the problem of getting the right data in the right format. However, a valuable assistant to find new problems, and new datasets to study, comes from the Kaggle platform (https://www.kaggle.com/).

The Kaggle platform was founded in 2010 as a platform for predictive modeling and analytics competitions on which companies and researchers post their data and statisticians and data miners from all over the world compete to produce the best models.

In this section, we show how to make a CNN for emotion detection from facial images. The train and test set of this example can be downloaded from https://inclass.kaggle.com/c/facial-keypoints-detector/data.

Please note that you can login and download the data using Facebook, Google+ or Yahoo. Alternatively, you will have to create an account and you can download the dataset.

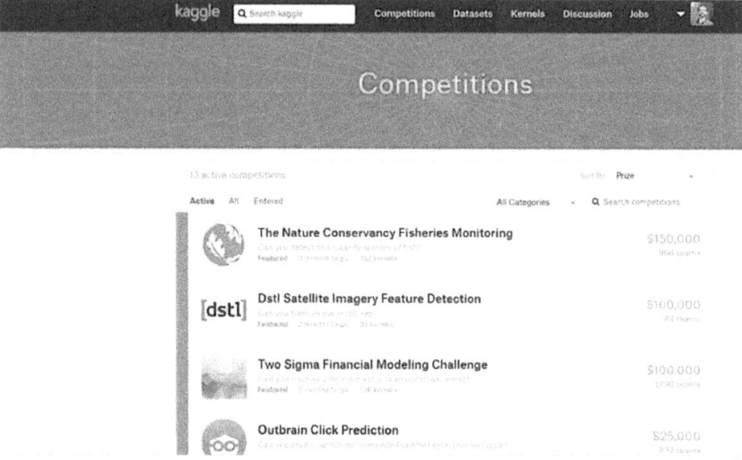

Figure 3.9 The Kaggle competition page

The train set consists of 3,761 grayscale images of 48x48 pixels in size and a 3,761 label set of seven elements each.

Each element encodes an emotional stretch, 0 = anger, 1 = disgust, 2 = fear, 3 = happy, 4 = sad, 5 = surprise, 6 = neutral.

In a classic Kaggle competition, the set of labels obtained from the test set must be evaluated by subjecting it to the platform. In this example, we will train a neural network from a training set, after which we will evaluate the model on a single image.

Before starting the CNN implementation, we'll look at the downloaded data by implementing a simple procedure.

Import the libraries with the following code:

```
import numpy as np
from matplotlib import pyplot as plt
import EmotionDetectorUtils
```

Please note that there is a dependency on EmotionDetectorUtils and EmotionDetectorUtils uses pandas package to execute these codes. Now to install the pandas package use the following command on terminal on Ubuntu:

```
sudo apt-get update
sudo apt-get install python-pip
sudo pip install numpy
sudo pip install pandas
sudo apt-get install python-pandas
```

The read_data function allows you to build all the datasets starting with the downloaded data. You can find it in the EmotionDetectorUtils library, which you can download in the code repository for this book:

```
FLAGS = tf.flags.FLAGS
tf.flags.DEFINE_string("data_dir", "EmotionDetector/", "Path to data files")
train_images, train_labels, valid_images, valid_labels, test_images = EmotionDetectorUtils.read_data(FLAGS.data_dir)
```

Then print the shape of the training images set and test sets:

```
print "train images shape = ",train_images.shape
print "test labels shape = ",test_images.shape
```

Display the first image of the training set and its correct label:

```
image_0 = train_images[0]
label_0 = train_labels[0]
print "image_0 shape = ",image_0.shape
print "label set = ",label_0
image_0 = np.resize(image_0,(48,48))
plt.imshow(image_0, cmap='Greys_r')
plt.show()
```

There are 3761 grayscale images of 48x48 pixels size:

train images shape = (3,761, 48, 48, 1)

There are 3761 class labels, each class contains seven elements:

train labels shape = (3,761, 7)

The test set is formed by 1312 grayscale images of 48x48 pixel size:

test labels shape = (1,312, 48, 48, 1)

A single image has the following shape:

image_0 shape = (48, 48, 1)

The label set for the first image is:

label set = [0. 0. 0. 1. 0. 0. 0.]

It corresponds to a happy emotional stretch, that we visualize in the following matplot figure:

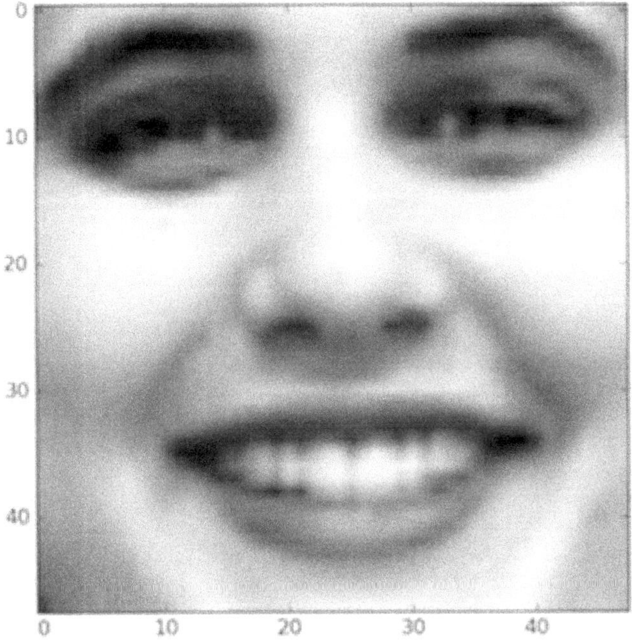

Figure 3.10 The first image from the emotion detection face dataset

We shall now proceed to study the CNN architecture. The following figure shows how the data flows in the CNN that will be implemented:

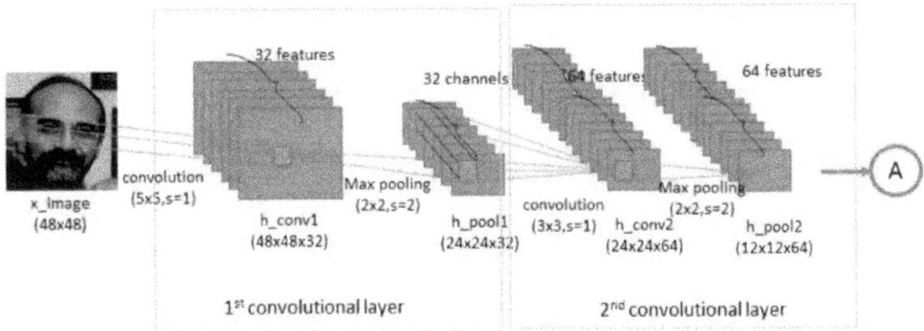

Figure 3.11 The first two convolutional layers of the implemented CNN

The network has two convolutional layers, two fully-connected layers and finally a softmax classification layer. The input image

(48 pixel) is processed in the first convolutional layer using 5x5 convolutional kernels. This results in 32 features, one for each filter used. The images are also downsampled by a max-pooling operation, to decrease the images from 48x48 to 24x24 pixels. These 32 smaller images are then processed by a second convolutional layer; this results in 64 new features (see the preceding figure). The resulting images are downsampled again to 12x12 pixels, by a second pooling operation.

The output of this second pooling layer is formed by 64 images of 12x12 pixels each. These are then flattened to a single vector of length 12x12x64 = 9,126, which is used as the input to a fully-connected layer with 256 neurons. This feeds into another fully-connected layer with 10 neurons, one for each of the classes, which is used to determine the class of the image, that is, which decodes the emotion in depicted in the image.

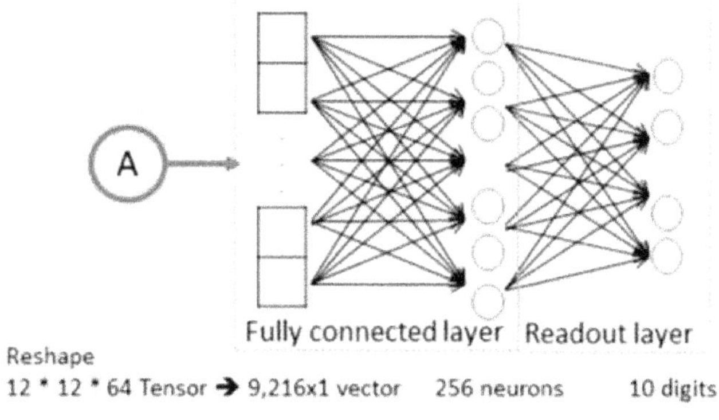

Figure 3.12 The last two layers of the implemented CNN

Let's go onto the weights and bias definition. The following data structure, represents the definition of the network's weights and summarizes what we have previously described:

```
weights = {
'wc1': weight_variable([5, 5, 1, 32], name="W_conv1"),
```

```
'wc2': weight_variable([3, 3, 32, 64],name="W_conv2"),
'wf1': weight_variable
([(IMAGE_SIZE / 4) * (IMAGE_SIZE / 4) * 64,
256],name="W_fc1"),
'wf2': weight_variable([256, NUM_LABELS], name="W_fc2")
}
```

Note again, that the convolutional filters are randomly chosen, so the classification is done randomly:

```
def weight_variable(shape, stddev=0.02, name=None):
initial = tf.truncated_normal(shape, stddev=stddev)
if name is None:
return tf.Variable(initial)
else:
return tf.get_variable(name, initializer=initial)
```

In a similar way, we have defined bias_variable:

```
biases = {
'bc1': bias_variable([32], name="b_conv1"),
'bc2': bias_variable([64], name="b_conv2"),
'bf1': bias_variable([256], name="b_fc1"),
'bf2': bias_variable([NUM_LABELS], name="b_fc2")
}
def bias_variable(shape, name=None):
initial = tf.constant(0.0, shape=shape)
if name is None:
return tf.Variable(initial)
else:
return tf.get_variable(name, initializer=initial)
```

An optimizer must propagate the error back through the CNN using the chain rule of differentiation and update the filter weights to improve the classification error. The error between the predicted and true class of the input image is measured by the implemented loss function. It takes in the input the predicted output of the pred model to the desired label output:

```
def loss(pred, label):
cross_entropy_loss=
tf.nn.softmax_cross_entropy_with_logits(pred, label)
cross_entropy_loss= tf.reduce_mean(cross_entropy_loss)
reg_losses = tf.add_n(tf.get_collection("losses"))
return cross_entropy_loss + REGULARIZATION * reg_losses
```

The tf.nn.softmax_cross_entropy_with_logits(pred, label) function computes the cross_entropy_loss of the result after applying the softmax function (but it does it altogether in a more mathematically careful way). It's like the result of:

```
a = tf.nn.softmax(x)
b = cross_entropy(a)
```

We calculate the cross_entropy_loss function for each of the classified images so that we'll have a measure of how well the model performs on each image individually.

We take the cross-entropy 's average for the classified images:

```
cross_entropy_loss= tf.reduce_mean(cross_entropy_loss)
```

To prevent overfitting, we use L2 regularization that consists of inserting an additional term to the cross_entropy_loss function:

```
reg_losses = tf.add_n(tf.get_collection("losses"))
return cross_entropy_loss + REGULARIZATION * reg_losses
```

Where:

```
def add_to_regularization_loss(W, b):
tf.add_to_collection("losses", tf.nn.l2_loss(W))
tf.add_to_collection("losses", tf.nn.l2_loss(b))
```

See http://www.kdnuggets.com/2015/04/preventing-overfitting-neural-networks.html/2 for further reference.

We built the network's weights and bias and their optimization procedure. However, like all the implemented networks, we must start the implementation by importing all necessary libraries:

```
import tensorflow as tf
import numpy as np
import os, sys, inspect
from datetime import datetime
import EmotionDetectorUtils
```

We set the paths for storing the dataset on the computer, and the network parameters with the following code:

```
FLAGS = tf.flags.FLAGS
tf.flags.DEFINE_string("data_dir",
"EmotionDetector/", "Path to data files")
tf.flags.DEFINE_string("logs_dir",
"logs/EmotionDetector_logs/", "Path to where log files are to be
saved")
tf.flags.DEFINE_string("mode", "train", "mode: train (Default)/
test")
BATCH_SIZE = 128
LEARNING_RATE = 1e-3
MAX_ITERATIONS = 1001
REGULARIZATION = 1e-2
IMAGE_SIZE = 48
NUM_LABELS = 7
```

VALIDATION_PERCENT = 0.1

The emotion_cnn function implements our model:

```
def emotion_cnn(dataset):
with tf.name_scope("conv1") as scope:
tf.summary.histogram("W_conv1", weights['wc1'])
tf.summary.histogram("b_conv1", biases['bc1'])
conv_1 = tf.nn.conv2d(dataset, weights['wc1'],
strides=[1, 1, 1, 1], padding="SAME")
h_conv1 = tf.nn.bias_add(conv_1, biases['bc1'])
h_1 = tf.nn.relu(h_conv1)
h_pool1 = max_pool_2x2(h_1)
add_to_regularization_loss(weights['wc1'], biases['bc1'])
with tf.name_scope("conv2") as scope:
tf.summary.histogram("W_conv2",          weights['wc2'])
tf.summary.histogram("b_conv2",     biases[     conv_2     =
tf.nn.conv2d(h_pool1, weights['wc2'],
strides=[1, 1, 1, 1], padding="SAME")
h_conv2 = tf.nn.bias_add(conv_2, biases['bc2'])
h_2 = tf.nn.relu(h_conv2)
h_pool2 = max_pool_2x2(h_2)
add_to_regularization_loss(weights['wc2'], biases['bc2'])
with tf.name_scope("fc_1") as scope:
prob=0.5
image_size = IMAGE_SIZE / 4
h_flat = tf.reshape(h_pool2, [-1, image_size * image_size * 64])
tf.summary.histogram("W_fc1", weights['wf1'])
tf.summary.histogram("b_fc1", biases['bf1'])
h_fc1 = tf.nn.relu(tf.matmul
(h_flat, weights['wf1']) + biases['bf1'])
h_fc1_dropout = tf.nn.dropout(h_fc1, prob)
with tf.name_scope("fc_2") as scope:
tf.summary.histogram("W_fc2", weights['wf2'])
tf.summary.histogram("b_fc2", biases['bf2'])
```

```
pred = tf.matmul(h_fc1_dropout, weights['wf2']) + biases['bf2']
return pred
```

We defined a main function where we'll define the dataset, the input and output placeholder variables and the main session to start the training procedure:

```
def main(argv=None):
```

The first operation in this function is to load the dataset for the training and validation phase. We'll use the training set to teach the classifier to recognize the to-be-predicted labels, and the we'll use the validation set to estimate the classifier performance:

```
train_images,
train_labels,
valid_images,
valid_labels,
test_images =
EmotionDetectorUtils.read_data(FLAGS.data_dir)
print "Train size: %s" % train_images.shape[0]
print 'Validation size: %s' % valid_images.shape[0]
print "Test size: %s" % test_images.shape[0]
```

We define the placeholder variable for the input images. This allows us to change the images that are input to the TensorFlow graph. The datatype is set to float32 and the shape is set to [None, IMG_SIZE, IMAGE_SIZE, 1], where None means that the tensor may hold an arbitrary number of images with each image

being img_size pixels high and img_size pixels wide and 1 is the number of color channels:

```
input_dataset = tf.placeholder(tf.float32,
[None,
IMAGE_SIZE,
IMAGE_SIZE, 1],name="input")
```

Next, we have the placeholder variable for the true labels associated with the images that were input in the input_dataset placeholder variable. The shape of this placeholder variable is [None, NUM_LABELS] which means it may hold an arbitrary number of labels and each label is a vector of length NUM_LABELS, which is 7 in this case:

```
input_labels = tf.placeholder(tf.float32,
[None, NUM_LABELS])
```

The global_step variable keeps track of the number of optimization iterations performed so far. We want to save this variable with all the other TensorFlow variables in the checkpoints. Note that trainable=False which means that TensorFlow will not try to optimize this variable:

```
global_step = tf.Variable(0, trainable=False)
```

And the following variable, dropout_prob, for dropout optimization:

```
dropout_prob = tf.placeholder(tf.float32)
```

Now create the neural network for the test phase. The emotion_cnn() function returns the predicted pred class labels for the input_dataset variable:

pred = emotion_cnn(input_dataset)

The output_pred variable is the predictions for the test and validation, which we'll compute in the running session:

output_pred = tf.nn.softmax(pred,name="output")

The loss_val variable contains the error between the pred predicted class and the true class of the input

image (input_labels):
loss_val = loss(pred, input_labels)

The train_op variable defines the optimizer used to minimize the cost function. In this case again we use

AdamOptimizer:
train_op = tf.train.AdamOptimizer
(LEARNING_RATE).minimize
(loss_val, global_step)
And summary_op for TensorBoard visualizations:
summary_op = tf.merge_all_summaries()

Once the graph has been created, we need to create a TensorFlow session which is used to execute the graph:

with tf.Session() as sess:
sess.run(tf.global_variables_initializer())
summary_writer = tf.summary.FileWriter(FLAGS.logs_dir, sess.graph_def)

We define a saver variable to restore the model:

```
saver = tf.train.Saver()

ckpt = tf.train.get_checkpoint_state(FLAGS.logs_dir)
if ckpt and ckpt.model_checkpoint_path:
saver.restore(sess, ckpt.model_checkpoint_path)
print "Model Restored!"
```

Get a batch of training examples, batch_image now holds a batch of images and batch_label are the true labels for those images:

```
for step in xrange(MAX_ITERATIONS):
batch_image, batch_label = get_next_batch(train_images,
train_labels,
step)
```

We put the batch into a dict variable with the proper names for placeholder variables in the TensorFlow graph:

```
feed_dict = {input_dataset: batch_image,
input_labels: batch_label}
```

We run the optimizer using this batch of training data; TensorFlow assigns the variables in feed_dict_train to the placeholder variables and then runs the optimizer:

```
sess.run(train_op, feed_dict=feed_dict
if step % 10 == 0:
train_loss,
summary_str =
sess.run([loss_val,summary_op],
feed_dict=feed_dict)
summary_writer.add_summary(summary_str,
global_step=step)
print "Training Loss: %f" % train_loss
```

When the running step is a multiple of 100, we run the trained model on the validation set:

```
if step % 100 == 0:
valid_loss =
sess.run(loss_val,
feed_dict={input_dataset:
valid_images,
input_labels:
valid_labels})
Print the Loss value:
print "%s Validation Loss: %f"
% (datetime.now(), valid_loss)
```

At the end of the training session the model is saved:

```
saver.save(sess, FLAGS.logs_dir
+         'model.ckpt',
global_step=step)
if __name__ == "__main__":
```

Now we report the resulting output. As you can see the loss function decreased during the following simulation:

```
>>>
Train size: 3761
Validation size: 417
Test size: 1312
2016-11-05 22:39:36.645682 Validation Loss: 1.962719
2016-11-05 22:42:58.951699 Validation Loss: 1.822431
2016-11-05 22:46:55.144483 Validation Loss: 1.335237
2016-11-05 22:50:17.677074 Validation Loss: 1.111559
2016-11-05 22:53:30.999141 Validation Loss: 0.999061
```

```
2016-11-05 22:56:53.256991 Validation Loss: 0.931223
2016-11-05 23:00:06.530139 Validation Loss: 0.911489
2016-11-05 23:03:15.351156 Validation Loss: 0.818303
2016-11-05 23:06:26.575298 Validation Loss: 0.824178
2016-11-05 23:09:40.136353 Validation Loss: 0.803449
2016-11-05 23:12:50.769527 Validation Loss: 0.851074
>>>
```

4

Optimizing TensorFlow Autoencoders

A big problem that plagues all supervised learning systems is the so-called curse of dimensionality; a progressive decline in performance with an increase in the input space dimension. This occurs because the number of necessary samples to obtain a sufficient sampling of the input space increases exponentially with the number of dimensions. To overcome these problems, some optimizing networks have been developed.

The first are autoencoder networks, these are designed and trained for transforming an input pattern in itself, so that, in the presence of a degraded or incomplete version of an input pattern, it is possible to obtain the original pattern. The network is trained to create output data, like those presented in the entrance, and the hidden layer stores the data compressed, that is, a compact representation that captures the fundamental characteristics of the input data.

The second optimizing networks are Boltzmann machines. These types of networks consist of an input/output visible layer, and one hidden layer. The connections between the visible layer and the hidden one are non-directional: data can travel in both directions, visible-hidden and hidden-visible, and the different neuronal units can be fully or partially connected.

Autoencoders can be compared with Principal Component Analysis (PCA), which is used to represent a given input using fewer dimensions than originally present. In this chapter, we'll focus only on autoencoders.

4.1 Introducing autoencoders

An autoencoder is a network with three or more layers, where the input layer and the output have the same number of neurons, and those intermediate (hidden) layers have a lower number of neurons. The network is trained to simply reproduce in output, for each input data, the same pattern of activity in the input.

The following figure shows how an auto encoder typically works: it reconstructs the received input through two phases, an encoding phase, that corresponds to a dimensional reduction for the original input, and a decoding phase, capable of reconstructing the original input from the encoded (compressed)

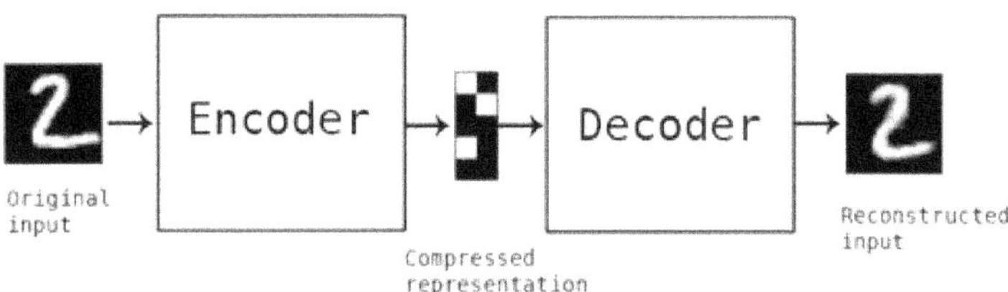

Figure 4.1 Encoder and decoder phase in autoencoder

4.2 Implementing an autoencoder

Training an autoencoder is basically a simple process. It is a neural network whose output is same as the input. The basic architecture of the autoencoder is as follows.

There is an input layer, which is followed by a few hidden layers, and then, after a certain depth, the hidden layers follow the reverse architecture until we reach a point where the final layer is the same as the input layer. We pass data into the network whose embedding we wish to learn.

In this example, we use the images input by the MNIST dataset. We begin our implementation by importing all the main libraries:

```
import tensorflow as tf
import numpy as np
import matplotlib.pyplot as plt
import mnist_data
```

We then prepare the MNIST dataset. We use the input_data function to load and set up the data:

```
from tensorflow.examples.tutorials.mnist import input_data
mnist = input_data.read_data_sets
("MNIST_data/",one_hot=True)
```

Then configure the network parameters:

```
learning_rate = 0.01
training_epochs = 10
batch_size = 256
display_step = 1
examples_to_show = 4
```

The sizes of the hidden features are as follows:

```
n_hidden_1 = 256
n_hidden_2 = 128
```

The size of the input images is as follows:

```
n_input = 784
```

The final size corresponds to 28x28=784 pixels.

Define a placeholder variable for the input images. The data type for this tensor is set to float and the shape is set to [None, n_input]. Defining the None parameter, the tensor may hold an arbitrary number of images:

```
X = tf.placeholder("float", [None, n_input])
```

Then, we can define the weights and biases of the network. The weights data structure contains the definition of the weights for the encoder and decoder. Notice that weights are chosen using tf.random_normal, which returns random values with a normal distribution:

```
weights = {
'encoder_h1': tf.Variable\
(tf.random_normal([n_input, n_hidden_1])),
'encoder_h2': tf.Variable\
(tf.random_normal([n_hidden_1, n_hidden_2])),
'decoder_h1': tf.Variable\
(tf.random_normal([n_hidden_2, n_hidden_1])),
'decoder_h2': tf.Variable\
(tf.random_normal([n_hidden_1, n_input])),
}
```

Similarly, we have defined the network's bias:

```
biases = {
'encoder_b1': tf.Variable\
(tf.random_normal([n_hidden_1])),
'encoder_b2': tf.Variable\
(tf.random_normal([n_hidden_2])),
'decoder_b1': tf.Variable\
(tf.random_normal([n_hidden_1])),
'decoder_b2': tf.Variable\
(tf.random_normal([n_input])),
```

}

We split the network modeling into two complementary, fully connected networks: an encoder and a decoder.

The encoder encodes the data; it takes as input an image, X, of the MNIST dataset, and performs the data encoding:

```
encoder_in = tf.nn.sigmoid(tf.add\
(tf.matmul(X,\
weights['encoder_h1']),\
biases['encoder_b1']))
```

The input data encoding is simply a matrix multiplication operation. The input data, X, of dimension 784 is reduced to a lower dimension, 256, using a matrix multiplication:

*(W*x + b)= encoder_in*

Here, W is the weight tensor, encoder_h1, and b is the bias tensor, encoder_b1.

Through this operation, we have coded the initial image into a useful input to the autoencoder. The second step of the encoding procedure consists of data compression.

The data represented by the input encoder_in tensor is reduced to a smaller size by means of a second matrix multiplication operation:

```
encoder_out = tf.nn.sigmoid(tf.add\
(tf.matmul(encoder_in,\
weights['encoder_h2']),\
biases['encoder_b2']))
```

The input data, encoder_in, of dimension 256, is then compressed to a lower tensor of size 128:

(W * encoder_in + b) = encoder_out

Here, W stands for the weight tensor, encoder_h2, while b stands for the bias tensor, encoder_b2.

Notice that the activation function we used for the encoder phase is the sigmoid.

The decoder performs the inverse operation of the encoder. It decompresses the input to obtain an output of the same size of the network input. The first step of the procedure is to transform the encoder_out tensor of size 128 to a tensor of intermediate representation, of size 256:

```
decoder_in = tf.nn.sigmoid(tf.add
(tf.matmul(encoder_out,\
weights['decoder_h1']),\
biases['decoder_b1']))
```

In the formulas, this means the following:

*(W * encoder_out + b) = decoder_in*

Here, W is the weight tensor, decoder_h1, of size 256x128, and b is the bias tensor, decoder_b1, of size 256.

The final operation of decoding is to decompress the data from its intermediate representation (of size 256), to a final representation (of size 784), which, as you will recall, is the size of the original data:

```
decoder_out = tf.nn.sigmoid(tf.add \
(tf.matmul(decoder_in,\
```

weights['decoder_h2']),
biases['decoder_b2']))
The y_pred parameter is set equal to decoder_out:
y_pred = decoder_out

The network will learn if the input data, X, is equal to the decoded data, so we define the following:

y_true = X

The point of the autoencoder is to create a reduction matrix that is good at reconstructing the original data. Thus, we want to minimize the cost function. Then we define the cost function as the mean squared error between y_true and y_pred:

cost = tf.reduce_mean(tf.pow(y_true - y_pred, 2))

To optimize the cost function, we use following the RMSPropOptimizer class:

optimizer = tf.train.RMSPropOptimizer (learning_rate) .minimize(cost)

Then we prepare to launch the session:

init = tf.global_variables_initializer()
with tf.Session() as sess:
sess.run(init)

Set the size of batch images to train the network:

total_batch = int(mnist.train.num_examples/batch_size)

Start with the training cycle (the number of training_epochs is set to 10):

```
for epoch in range(training_epochs):
While looping over all batches:
for i in range(total_batch):
batch_xs, batch_ys =\
mnist.train.next_batch(batch_size)
```

We run the optimization procedure, feeding the execution graph with the batch set, batch_xs:

```
_, c = sess.run([optimizer, cost],\
feed_dict={X: batch_xs})
Display results per epoch step:
if epoch % display_step == 0:
print("Epoch:", '%04d' % (epoch+1),
"cost=", "{:.9f}".format(c))
print("Optimization Finished!")
```

Finally, we test the model, applying the encode or decode procedure. We feed the model with a subset of images, where the value of example_to_show is set to 4:

```
encode_decode = sess.run(y_pred, feed_dict=\
{X: mnist.test.images[:examples_to_show]})
```

We compare the original images with their reconstructions, using matplotlib capabilities:

```
f, a = plt.subplots(2, 4, figsize=(10, 5))
for i in range(examples_to_show):
a[0][i].imshow(np.reshape(mnist.test.images[i], (28, 28)))
a[1][i].imshow(np.reshape(encode_decode[i], (28, 28)))
f.show()
plt.draw()
plt.show()
```

Running the session, we should have an output as follows:

Extracting MNIST_data/train-images-idx3-ubyte.gz
Extracting MNIST_data/train-labels-idx1-ubyte.gz
Extracting MNIST_data/t10k-images-idx3-ubyte.gz
Extracting MNIST_data/t10k-labels-idx1-ubyte.gz
('Epoch:', '0001', 'cost=', '0.196781039')
('Epoch:', '0002', 'cost=', '0.157454371')
('Epoch:', '0003', 'cost=', '0.139842913')
('Epoch:', '0004', 'cost=', '0.132784918')
('Epoch:', '0005', 'cost=', '0.123214975')
('Epoch:', '0006', 'cost=', '0.117614307')
('Epoch:', '0007', 'cost=', '0.111050725')
('Epoch:', '0008', 'cost=', '0.111332968')
('Epoch:', '0009', 'cost=', '0.107702859')
('Epoch:', '0010', 'cost=', '0.106899358')
Optimization Finished!

Then we display the results; the first row has the original images, while the second row has the decoded images:

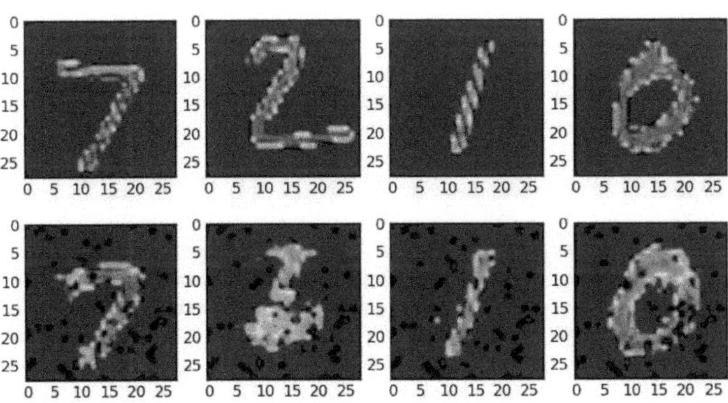

Figure 4.2 Original and decoded images

4.3 Improving autoencoder robustness

A successful strategy we can take to improve the model's robustness is to introduce a noise in the encoding phase. Indeed, we call a denoising autoencoder a stochastic version of an autoencoder, in which the input is stochastically corrupted, but the uncorrupted version of the same input is used as a target for the decoding phase.

Intuitively, a denoising autoencoder does two things: first, it tries to encode the input, preserving the concerning information, and then it seeks to nullify the effect of the corruption process applied to the same input.In the following section, we'll show an implementation of a denoising autoencoder.

4.4 Building denoising autoencoders

The network architecture is very simple. An input image, of size 784 pixels, is stochastically corrupted, and then it is dimensionally reduced by an encoding network layer. The reduction step is from 784 to 256 pixels.

In the decoding phase, we prepare the network for output, re-changing the original image size from 256 to 784 pixels.

As usual, we start loading all the necessary libraries to our implementation:

```
import numpy as np
import tensorflow as tf
import matplotlib.pyplot as plt
from tensorflow.examples.tutorials.mnist import input_data
```

Set the basic network parameters:

```
n_input = 784
```

```
n_hidden_1 = 256
n_hidden_2 = 256
n_output       = 784
```

We also set the session's parameters:

```
epochs  = 110
batch_size = 100
disp_step       = 10
```

We build the training and test sets. We again use the input_data feature imported from the tensorflow.examples.tutorials.mnist library present in the installation package:

```
print ("PACKAGES LOADED")
mnist = input_data.read_data_sets('data/', one_hot=True)
trainimg        = mnist.train.images
trainlabel = mnist.train.labels
testimg  = mnist.test.images
testlabel        = mnist.test.labels
print ("MNIST LOADED")
```

Let's define a placeholder variable for the input images. The data type is set to float and the shape is set to [None, n_input]. The None parameter means that the tensor may hold an arbitrary number of images, and the size per image is n_input:

```
x = tf.placeholder("float", [None, n_input])
```

Next, we have a placeholder variable for the true labels associated with the images that were input in the placeholder variable x. The shape of this placeholder variable is [None, n_output], which means it may hold an arbitrary number of labels, and each label is a vector of length n_output, which is 10 in this case:

```
y = tf.placeholder("float", [None, n_output])
```

To reduce overfitting, we'll apply a dropout before the encoding and decoding procedure, so we must define a placeholder for the probability that a neuron's output is kept during the dropout:

```
dropout_keep_prob = tf.placeholder("float")
```

On these definitions, we fix the weights and network's biases:

```
weights = {
'h1': tf.Variable(tf.random_normal([n_input, n_hidden_1])),
'h2': tf.Variable(tf.random_normal([n_hidden_1, n_hidden_2])),
'out': tf.Variable(tf.random_normal([n_hidden_2, n_output]))
}
biases = {
'b1': tf.Variable(tf.random_normal([n_hidden_1])),
'b2': tf.Variable(tf.random_normal([n_hidden_2])),
'out': tf.Variable(tf.random_normal([n_output]))
}
```

Weights and biases are chosen using tf.random_normal, which returns random values with a normal distribution.

The encoding phase takes as its input an image from the MNIST dataset, and then performs the data compression, applying a matrix multiplication operation:

```
encode_in = tf.nn.sigmoid\
(tf.add(tf.matmul\
(x, weights['h1']),\
biases['b1']))
encode_out = tf.nn.dropout\
(encode_in, dropout_keep_prob)
```

In the decoding phase, we apply the same procedure:

```
decode_in = tf.nn.sigmoid\
(tf.add(tf.matmul\
(encode_out, weights['h2']),\
biases['b2']))
```

The over-fitting reduction is made by a dropout procedure:

```
decode_out = tf.nn.dropout(decode_in,\
dropout_keep_prob)
```

Finally, we are ready to build the prediction tensor, y_pred:

```
y_pred = tf.nn.sigmoid\
(tf.matmul(decode_out,\
weights['out']) +\
biases['out'])
```

We then define a cost measure that is used to guide the variables optimization procedure:

```
cost = tf.reduce_mean(tf.pow(y_pred - y, 2))
```

We will minimize the cost function, using the RMSPropOptimizer class:

```
optmizer = tf.train.RMSPropOptimizer(0.01).minimize(cost)
```

Finally, we can initialize the defined variables:

```
init = tf.initialize_all_variables()
```

Set TensorFlow's running session:

```
with tf.Session() as sess:
sess.run(init)
print ("Start Training")
for epoch in range(epochs):
num_batch      = int(mnist.train.num_examples/batch_size)
total_cost = 0.
for i in range(num_batch):
```

For each training epoch, we select a smaller batch set from the training dataset:

```
batch_xs, batch_ys =\
mnist.train.next_batch(batch_size)
```

Here is the focal point: we randomly corrupt the batch_xs set using the random function by the numpy package previously imported:

```
batch_xs_noisy = batch_xs +\

0.3*np.random.randn(batch_size, 784)
```

We use these sets to feed the execution graph, and then to run the session (sess.run):

```
feeds = {x: batch_xs_noisy,\
y: batch_xs,\
dropout_keep_prob: 0.8}
sess.run(optmizer, feed_dict=feeds)
total_cost += sess.run(cost, feed_dict=feeds)
```

Every 10 epochs, the average cost value will be shown:

```
if epoch % disp_step == 0:
print ("Epoch %02d/%02d average cost: %.6f"
% (epoch, epochs, total_cost/num_batch))
```

Finally, we start to test the trained model:

```
print ("Start Test")
```

To make this, we randomically select an image from the test set:

```
randidx = np.random.randint\
(testimg.shape[0], size=1)
orgvec  = testimg[randidx, :]
testvec  = testimg[randidx, :]
label    = np.argmax(testlabel[randidx, :], 1)
print ("Test label is %d" % (label))
noisyvec = testvec + 0.3*np.random.randn(1, 784)
```

We then run the trained model on the selected image:

```
outvec = sess.run(y_pred,feed_dict={x: noisyvec,\

dropout_keep_prob: 1})
```

As we'll see, the following plotresult function will display the original image, the noisy image, and the predicted image:

```
plotresult(orgvec,noisyvec,outvec)

print ("restart Training")
```

Running the session, we should see a result like the following:

PACKAGES LOADED

Extracting data/train-images-idx3-ubyte.gz
Extracting data/train-labels-idx1-ubyte.gz
Extracting data/t10k-images-idx3-ubyte.gz
Extracting data/t10k-labels-idx1-ubyte.gz

MNIST LOADED

Start Training

For the sake of brevity, we only report the results after 10 epochs and after 100 epochs:

Epoch 00/100 average cost: 0.212313
Start Test
Test label is 6

The following are the original and the noisy images (the number 6, as you can see):

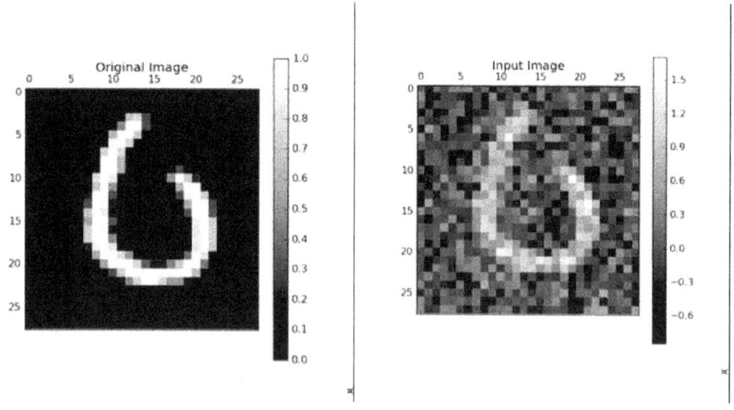

Figure 4.3 Original and noisy images

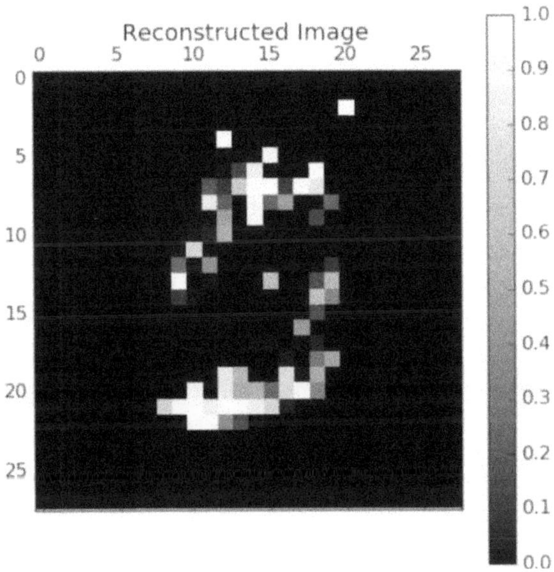

Figure 4.4 Reconstructed image

After 100 epochs, we have a better result:

Epoch 100/100 average cost: 0.018221
Start Test
Test label is 9

Again, the original and the noisy images:

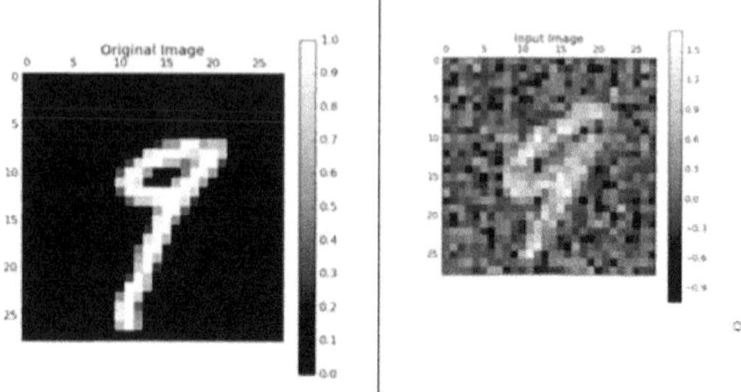

Figure 4.5 Original and noisy images

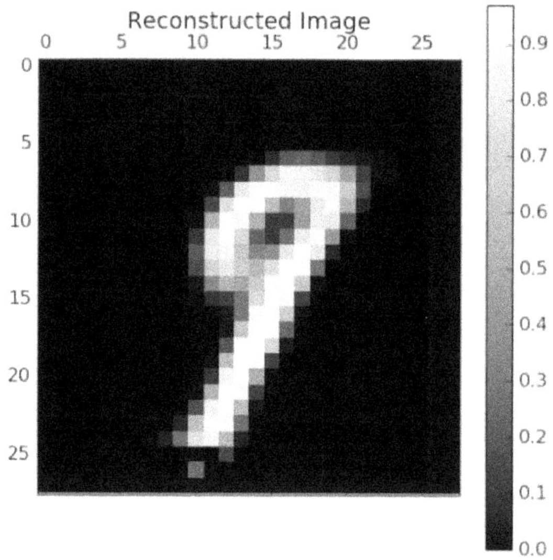

Figure 4.6 Reconstructed image

5

Recurrent Neural Networks

Deep learning architectures that are used widely nowadays are the so-called Recurrent Neural Networks (RNNs). The basic idea of RNNs is to make use of sequential type information in the input.

These networks are recurrent because they perform the same computations for all the elements of a sequence of inputs, and the output of each element depends, in addition to the current input, from all the previous computations.

RNNs have proved to have excellent performance in problems such as predicting the next character in a text or, similarly, the prediction of the next word sequence in a sentence.

However, they are also used for more complex problems, such as Machine Translation (MT). In this case, the network has as input a sequence of words in a source language, while the output will be the translated input sequence in a target language; finally, other applications of great importance in which the RNNs are widely used are speech recognition and also image recognition.

5.1 RNN basic concepts

Human beings don't start thinking from scratch, human minds have the so-called persistence of memory, namely, the ability to associate the past with recent information. Traditional neural networks, instead, ignore past events. Taking as an example, a movie's scenes classifier, it's not possible that a neural network uses past scenes to classify the current ones.

Trying to solve this problem, RNNs have been developed, in contrast with the Convolutional Neural Networks (CNNs), the RNNs are networks with a loop that allows the information to be persistent.

RNNs process a sequential input one at a time, updating a kind of vector state that contains information about all past elements of the sequence.

The following figure shows a neural network that takes as input a value of **X*t***, and then outputs an **O*t*** value:

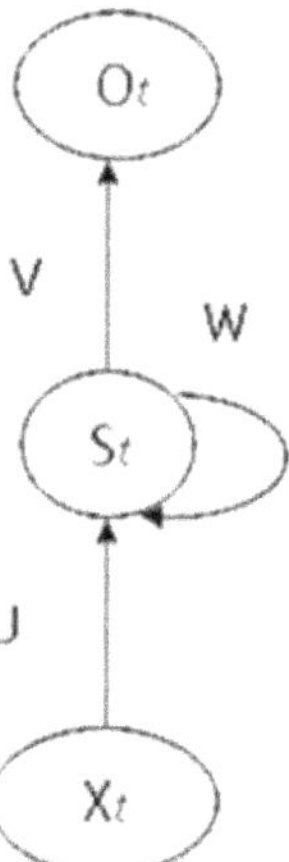

Figure 5.1 An RNN with its internal loop

5.2 RNNs at work

The state vector St is calculated starting from the current input and the state vector in previous time, through the U and W matrices:

$$S_t = f(U \cdot x_t + W \cdot s_{t-1})$$

f is a nonlinear function such as ***tanh or ReLU***. As you can see, the two terms in the function are added together before being processed by the function itself. Finally, Ot; is the network output, calculated using the matrix V:

$$O_t = V \cdot S_t$$

5.3 Unfolding an RNN

The next figure shows an unfolded version of an RNN, obtained by unrolling the network structure for the entire input sequence, at different and discrete times. It is immediately clear that it is different from the typical multi-level neural networks, which use different parameters at each level; an **RNN** uses the same parameters, ***U, V, W***, for each instant of time.

Indeed, RNNs perform the same computation at each instance, on different inputs of the same sequence. Sharing the same parameters, also, an **RNN** strongly reduces the number of parameters that the network must learn during the training phase, thus also improving the training times.

Regarding this unfolded version, it is evident how through the backpropagation algorithm with only a small change, you can train networks of this type.

In fact, because the parameters are shared for each instant time, the computed gradient depends on the current computation, but also on the previous ones.

For example, to calculate the gradient (at a time t = 4) it is necessary to back propagate the computed gradient for three instants of time preceding and then sum the gradients thus obtained. In fact, an entire input sequence is typically considered to be a single element of the training set. Therefore, if the total error is simply the sum of the errors at each instant of time (for each element of the input sequence) as a result, the error gradient turns out to be the sum of the error gradients at each instant of time.

This procedure is called the **Backpropagation Through Time (BPTT).**

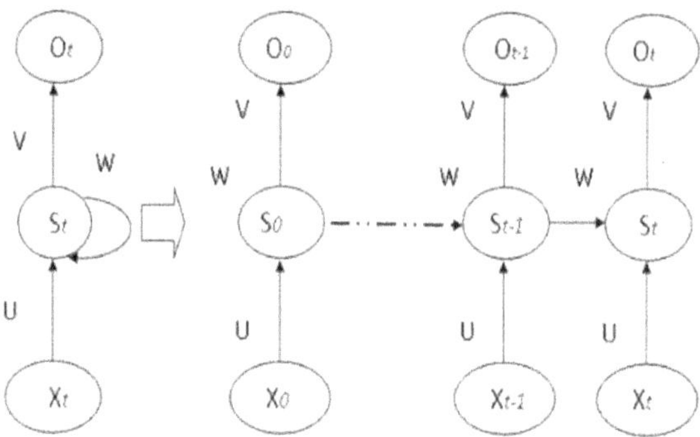

Figure 5.2 Unrolled version of an RNN

5.4 The vanishing gradient problem

In backpropagation algorithm, the weights are adjusted in proportion to the gradient error, and for the way in which the gradients are computed. Let's check the following:

If the weights are small, it can lead to a situation called vanishing gradients where the gradient signal gets so small that learning either becomes very slow or stops working altogether. This is often referred to as vanishing gradients.
If the weights in this matrix are large it can lead to a situation where the gradient signal is so large that it can cause learning to diverge. This is often referred to as exploding gradients.

The vanishing-exploding gradient problem also afflicts RNNs. In fact, the BPTT rolls out the RNN creating a very deep feed-forward neural network. The impossibility of having a long-term context by the RNN is due precisely to this phenomenon, if the gradient vanishes or explodes within a few layers, the network will not be able to learn high temporal distance relationships between the data.

The following figure shows schematically what happens; the computed and back propagated gradient tend to decrease (or increase) at each instant of time and then, after a certain number of instants of time, tend to converge to zero (or explode to infinity):

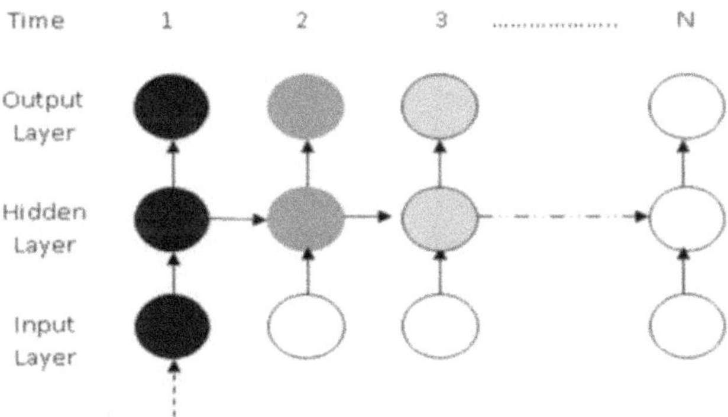

Figure 5.3 Vanishing gradient problem in RNNs

To overcome the vanishing-exploding problem, various extensions of the basic RNN model have been proposed, one of these, is represented, for example, by Long Short Term Memory (LSTM) networks that will be introduced in the next section.

5.5 LSTM networks

Long Short Term Memory (LSTM) is a special Recurrent Neural Network architecture, which was originally conceived by Hochreiter and Schmidhuber in 1997. This type of neural network has been recently rediscovered in the context of deep learning, because it is free from the problem of vanishing gradients, and offers excellent results and performance. The networks that are LSTM-based are ideal for prediction and classification of temporal sequences, and are replacing many traditional approaches to deep learning.

LSTM is a network that is composed of cells (LSTM blocks) linked to each other. Each LSTM block contains three types of gate: Input gate, Output gate, and Forget gate, respectively, which implement the functions of writing, reading, and resetting on the cell memory. These gates are not binary, but analogical (generally managed by a sigmoidal activation function mapped in the range [0, 1], where 0 indicates total inhibition, and 1 shows the total activation).

The presence of these gates, allows LSTM cells to remember information for an indefinite time; in fact, if the following Input gate is the activation threshold, the cell will retain the previous state, and if the current state is enabled, it will be combined with the input value. As the name suggests, the Forget gate resets the current state of the cell (when its value is cleared to 0), and the Output gate decides whether the value in the cell must be carried out or not.

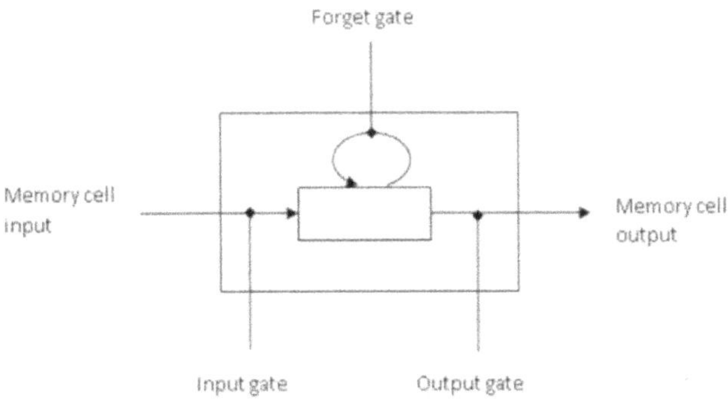

Figure 5.4 Block diagram of an LSTM cell

5.6 An image classifier with RNNs

At this point we introduce our implementation of a recurrent model including LSTMs blocks for an image classification problem. The dataset we used is the well known MNIST.

The implemented model is composed of a single LSTM layer followed by a reduce mean operation and a softmax layer, as illustrated in the following figure:

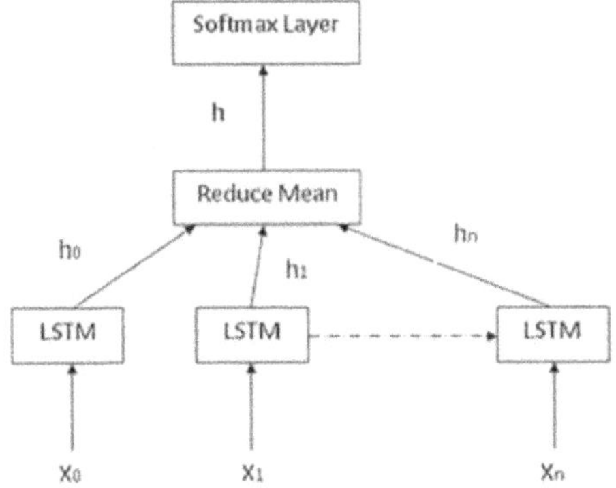

Figure 5.5 Dataflow in an RNN architecture

The following code computes the mean of elements across dimensions of a tensor and reduces input_tensor along the dimensions given in axis. Unless keep_dims is true, the rank of the tensor is reduced by 1 for each entry in axis. If keep_dims is true, the reduced dimensions are retained with length 1: tf.reduce_mean *(input_tensor, axis=None, keep_dims=False, name=None, reduction_indices=None)*

If axis has no entries, all dimensions are reduced, and a tensor with a single element is returned.
For example:

```
#        'x' is [[1., 1.]
#        [2., 2.]]
tf.reduce_mean(x)==> 1.5
tf.reduce_mean(x,0)==> [1.5,1.5]
tf.reduce_mean(x,1)==> [1.,2.]
```

Thus, starting from an input sequence x0, x1,...xn, the memory cells in the LSTM layer will produce a representation sequence h0, h1,...hn.

This representation sequence is then averaged over all time steps resulting in the final representation h. Finally, this representation is fed to a softmax layer whose target is the class label associated with the input sequence.

Let's begin the implementation, with the usual importing of all dependencies:

```
import tensorflow as tf
from tensorflow.contrib import rnn
```

The imported rnn and rnn_cell are TensorFlow classes, described as follows:

The *rnn_cell* module provides a number of basic commonly used RNN cells, such as LSTM and a number of operators that allow us to add dropouts, projections, or embeddings for inputs then we load the MNIST dataset using the following library:

from tensorflow.examples.tutorials.mnist import input_data
mnist = input_data.read_data_sets("/tmp/data/", one_hot=True)

It might take minutes as it downloads the dataset from the Internet.

To classify the images using a Recurrent Neural Network, we must consider every image row as a sequence of pixels, because MNIST image shape is 28×28 pixels, we will then handle 28 sequences of 28 timesteps for every sample.

We then define the following parameters:

MNIST data input (image shape: 28×28)
n_input = 28
the timesteps
n_steps = 28

The number of features in the hidden layer:

n_hidden = 128
MNIST total classes (0-9 digits)
n_classes = 10

Here we define our parameters that we will be using in the learning process:

```
learning_rate = 0.001
training_iters = 100000
batch_size = 128
display_step = 10
```

Define our input data (the images) as x. The datatype for this tensor is set to float and the shape is set to [None, n_steps, n_input]. The None parameter means that the tensor may hold an arbitrary number of images: x = tf.placeholder("float", [None, n_steps, n_input])

Then we have the placeholder variable for the true labels associated with the images that were input in the placeholder variable x. The shape of this placeholder variable is [None, n_classes], which means it may hold an arbitrary number of labels and each label is a vector of length n_classes, which is 10 in this case:

```
Y = tf.placeholder("float", [None, n_classes]) weights = {
'out': tf.Variable(tf.random_normal([n_hidden, n_classes]))
}
biases = {
'out': tf.Variable(tf.random_normal([n_classes]))
}
```

We define the network through the RNN function:

```
def RNN (x, weights, biases):
```

We set the input x data shape to correctly match the RNN function requirements. Notice the following:

The current input data will be (batch_size, n_steps, n_input)
The required shape is a n_steps tensors list of shape (batch_size, n_input)

In order to do this, we must perform some transformations on the x input tensor. The first operation is to permutate a transposition of the current input data:

x = tf.transpose(x, [1, 0, 2])

This operation returns a (28,28,128) tensor from the (128,28,28) current input data. Then, reshape x:

x = tf.reshape(x, [-1, n_input])

It returns a n_steps × batch_size, n_input tensor. Split the x tensor to get the required list of n_steps tensors of shape (batch_size, n_input):

x = tf.split(axis=0, num_or_size_splits=n_steps, value=x)

To define our Recurrent Neural Network perform the following steps:

1. Define a single LSTM cell: The BasicLSTMCell method defines LSTM recurrent network cell. The forget_bias parameter is set to 1.0 to reduce the scale of forgetting in the beginning of the training:

lstm_cell = rnn_cell.BasicLSTMCell(n_hidden, forget_bias=1.0)

2. Build the network: The rnn() operation creates the compute nodes for a given amount of time steps:

outputs, states = rnn. static_rnn (lstm_cell, x, dtype=tf.float32)

This operation returns the LSTM cell outputs, where: outputs is a length and n_steps is a list of outputs (one for each input) states are the cell final states

The resulting tensor of the RNN function is a vector of length 10 for determining which of the 10 classes the input image belongs to:

return tf.matmul(outputs[-1], weights['out']) + biases['out']

We define the cost function and optimizer for the predictor:

pred = RNN(x, weights, biases)

We used softmax_cross_entropy_with_logits as a performance measure and reduce_mean to take the average of the cross-entropy for all the image classifications: New:

cost = tf.reduce_mean (tf.nn.softmax_cross_entropy_with_logits (logits=pred, labels=y))

Then we apply the AdamOptimizer algorithm to minimize the cross-entropy so it gets as close to zero as possible by changing the variables of the network layers:

*Optimizer = tf.train.AdamOptimizer\
(learning_rate=learning_rate) .minimize (cost)*

We define the accuracy that will be displayed during the computation:

correct_pred = tf.equal(tf.argmax(pred,1), tf.argmax(y,1))
accuracy = tf.reduce_mean(tf.cast(correct_pred, tf.float32))

We then initialize the variables:

init = tf.global_variables_initializer()

It's time to begin the training session--first, we make our session to use it to make our computations happen:

with tf.Session() as sess: sess.run(init)
step = 1
Build the batch sets until we reach the maximum training iterations:
*while step * batch_size < training_iters:*
batch_x, batch_y = mnist.train.next_batch(batch_size)
Reshape data to get 28 sequences of 28 elements:
batch_x = batch_x.reshape((batch_size, n_steps, n_input))

Run through our data in the sequential manner, we break them into pieces and every piece is sized by the batch size that we defined, and then we take every piece and feed it to our optimizer and calculate our accuracy and error and repeat it by feeding new chunks, and so on. In this process, our accuracy gets better the more we feed it: *sess.run(optimizer, feed_dict={x: batch_x, y: batch_y}) if step % display_step == 0:*
Compute the accuracy using the following code:
acc = sess.run(accuracy, feed_dict={x: batch_x, y: batch_y})
The loss value, on the other hand, can be calculated as follows:

```
loss = sess.run(cost, feed_dict={x: batch_x, y: batch_y})
```
Then we can display the accuracy as follows:
```
print("Iter " + str(step*batch_size) + ", Minibatch Loss= " +\
"{:.6f}".format(loss) + ", Training Accuracy= " +\
"{:.5f}".format(acc))
step += 1
print("Optimization Finished!")
```
Finally, we test the RNN model, on a subset (or batch set) of images:
```
test_len = 128
test_data = mnist.test.images[:test_len]\
.reshape((-1, n_steps, n_input))
test_label = mnist.test.labels[:test_len]
print("Testing Accuracy:",\
sess.run(accuracy, feed_dict={x: test_data, y: test_label}))
```

5.7 Bidirectional RNNs

Bidirectional RNNs are based on the idea that the output at time t may depend on previous and future elements in the sequence. To realize this, the output of two RNN must be mixed--one executes the process in a direction and the second runs the process in the opposite direction. The network splits neurons of a regular RNN into two directions, one for positive time direction (forward states), and another for negative time direction (backward states). By this structure, the output layer can get information from past and future states. The unrolled architecture of B-RNN is depicted in the following figure:

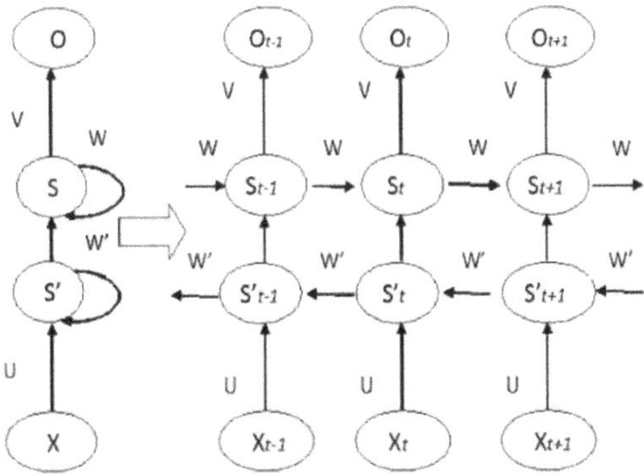

Figure 5.6 Unrolled bidirectional RNN

Let's see now, how to implement a B-RNN for an image classification problem. We begin by importing the needed library, notice that rnn and rnn_cell are TensorFlow libraries:

```
import tensorflow as tf
from tensorflow.contrib import rnn
import numpy as np
```

The network will classify the MNIST images, so we have to load them:

```
from tensorflow.examples.tutorials.mnist import input_data
mnist = input_data.read_data_sets("/tmp/data/", one_hot=True)
```

We then define the learning parameters:

```
learning_rate = 0.001
training_iters = 100000
batch_size = 128
display_step = 10
```

Next we configure the network's parameters:

```
n_input = 28
n_steps = 28
n_hidden = 128
n_classes = 10
```

Set up the placeholders, which we use to feed to our network. First, we define a placeholder variable for the input images. This allows us to change the images that are input to the TensorFlow graph. The datatype is set to float and the tensor's shape is set to [None, n_steps, n_input], None stands for a tensor that may hold an arbitrary number of images:

```
x = tf.placeholder("float", [None, n_steps, n_input])
```

Then we fix a second placeholder variable for the labels associated with the images that were input in the placeholder variable x. The shape of this placeholder variable is set to [None, n_classes], which means that it may hold an arbitrary number of labels and each label is a vector of length num_classes, which is 10 in this case:

```
y = tf.placeholder("float", [None, n_classes])
```

The first variable that must be optimized is weights and it is defined here as a TensorFlow variable that must be initialized with random uniform values and whose shape is [2*n_hidden, n_classes].

Here's the weights definition:

```
weights = {'out': tf.Variable(tf.random_normal([2*n_hidden,
n_classes])) }
```

Then we define the corresponding biases:

```
biases = {'out': tf.Variable(tf.random_normal([n_classes]))}
```

With the following BiRNN function we define the weights and network's biases:

```
def BiRNN(x, weights, biases):
```

To achieve this purpose, we apply the following sequence of tensor transformations:

```
x = tf.transpose(x, [1, 0, 2])
x = tf.reshape(x, [-1, n_input])
x = tf.split(axis=0, num_or_size_splits=n_steps, value=x)
```

Despite the previous model, we define two types of LSTM cells, a forward cell and a backward cell:

```
lstm_fw_cell = rnn_cell.BasicLSTMCell(n_hidden,
forget_bias=1.0)

lstm_bw_cell = rnn_cell.BasicLSTMCell(n_hidden,
forget_bias=1.0)
```

Then we build the bidirectional network using the following imported class rnn.bidirectional_rnn(). Similar to the unidirectional case, rnn.bidirectional_rnn() takes as input and builds independent forward and backward RNNs with the final forward and backward outputs depth-concatenated:

```
try:
outputs, _, _ = rnn. static_bidirectional_rnn
```

(lstm_fw_cell, lstm_bw_cell, x,dtype=tf.float32)
except Exception:
outputs = rnn. static_bidirectional_rnn
(lstm_fw_cell, lstm_bw_cell, x,dtype=tf.float32)

The input_size of forward and backward cells must match. Notice that outputs will have the following format:

[time][batch][cell_fw.output_size + cell_bw.output_size]

The BiRNN function returns an output tensor for determining which of the 10 classes the input image belongs to:

return tf.matmul(outputs[-1], weights['out']) + biases['out']

The value returned by the BiRNN function will then be passed to the pred tensor:

pred = BiRNN(x, weights, biases)

We have to compute the cross-entropy value for each classified image, because we must have a measure of how well the model works individually on each image.

Using the cross-entropy to guide the network's optimization procedure we need a single scalar value, so we simply take the cross-entropy average (tf.reduce_mean) evaluated for all the classified images:

New: cost = tf.reduce_mean
(tf.nn.softmax_cross_entropy_with_logits (logits=pred,
labels=y))

The obtained cost measure will be minimized by an optimizer variable. We use the AdamOptimizer, which is an advanced form of gradient descent:

optimizer = tf.train. AdamOptimizer \ (learning_rate = learning_rate) .minimize(cost)

We add performance measures to be able to display the progress during the training phase. It is a vector of

Booleans whether the predicted class equals the true class of each image:

correct_pred = tf.equal(tf.argmax(pred,1), tf.argmax(y,1))

The correct_pred variable is used here to compute the classification accuracy by first type-casting the vector of Booleans to float, so that false becomes 0 and true becomes 1, and then calculating the average of these numbers:

accuracy = tf.reduce_mean(tf.cast(correct_pred, tf.float32))

All the variables must be initialized before we start optimizing them:

init = tf.global_variables_initializer()

We then create a session, which will execute the graph:

with tf.Session() as sess:
sess.run(init)
step = 1

During the session, we get a batch of training examples:

```
while step * batch_size < training_iters:
```

The batch_x variable now holds a subset of training images and batch_y is a subset of true labels for those images:

```
batch_x, batch_y = mnist.train.next_batch(batch_size)
batch_x = batch_x.reshape((batch_size, n_steps, n_input))
```

We put the batch sets into feed_dict with the proper names for the placeholder variables, then we run the optimizer through sess.run:

```
sess.run(optimizer, feed_dict={x: batch_x, y: batch_y})
if step % display_step == 0:
```

We calculate the accuracy and the loss values on these sets:

```
acc = sess.run(accuracy,\
feed_dict={x: batch_x, y: batch_y})
loss = sess.run(cost,\
feed_dict={x: batch_x, y: batch_y})
print("Iter " + str(step*batch_size) +\
", Minibatch Loss= " +\
"{:.6f}".format(loss) + ", Training Accuracy= " +\
"{:.5f}".format(acc))
step += 1
print("Optimization Finished!")
```

At the end of the training session we get a batch of testing examples:

```
test_len = 128
test_data = mnist.test.images\
[:test_len].reshape((-1, n_steps, n_input))
test_label = mnist.test.labels[:test_len]
```

Finally, we can calculate and display the accuracy on this test set:

```
print("Testing Accuracy:",\
sess.run(accuracy, feed_dict={x: test_data, y: test_label}))
```

We show only an excerpt of the output. Here you can visualize the loss value and the accuracy evaluated on the batch sets:

Successfully downloaded train-images-idx3-ubyte.gz 9912422 bytes. Extracting /tmp/data/train-images-idx3-ubyte.gz Successfully downloaded train-labels-idx1-ubyte.gz 28881 bytes. Extracting /tmp/data/train-labels-idx1-ubyte.gz Successfully downloaded t10k-images-idx3-ubyte.gz 1648877 bytes. Extracting /tmp/data/t10k-images-idx3-ubyte.gz Successfully downloaded t10k-labels-idx1-ubyte.gz 4542 bytes. Extracting /tmp/data/t10k-labels-idx1-ubyte.gz Iter 12 Minibatch Loss= 1.877825, Training Accuracy= 0.34375

Iter 2560, Minibatch Loss= 1.582133, Training Accuracy= 0.45312
Iter 3840, Minibatch Loss= 1.172375, Training Accuracy= 0.53125
Iter 5120, Minibatch Loss= 0.942408, Training Accuracy= 0.67188
Iter 6400, Minibatch Loss= 0.678984, Training Accuracy= 0.73438
Iter 7680, Minibatch Loss= 1.089620, Training Accuracy= 0.64844
Iter 8960, Minibatch Loss= 0.658389, Training Accuracy= 0.79688
Iter 10240, Minibatch Loss= 0.576066, Training Accuracy= 0.82031
Iter 11520, Minibatch Loss= 0.404379, Training Accuracy= 0.92188

Iter 12800, Minibatch Loss= 0.627313, Training Accuracy= 0.79688
Iter 14080, Minibatch Loss= 0.447121, Training Accuracy= 0.87500
....
Iter 90880, Minibatch Loss= 0.048776, Training Accuracy= 1.00000
Iter 92160, Minibatch Loss= 0.096100, Training Accuracy= 0.98438
Iter 93440, Minibatch Loss= 0.059382, Training Accuracy= 0.98438
Iter 94720, Minibatch Loss= 0.088342, Training Accuracy= 0.97656
Iter 96000, Minibatch Loss= 0.083945, Training Accuracy= 0.98438
Iter 97280, Minibatch Loss= 0.077618, Training Accuracy= 0.97656
Iter 98560, Minibatch Loss= 0.141791, Training Accuracy= 0.93750
Iter 99840, Minibatch Loss= 0.064927, Training Accuracy= 0.98438
Optimization Finished!

5.8 Text prediction

Language computational models based on RNNs are nowadays among the most successful techniques for statistical language modeling. They can be easily applied in a wide range of tasks, including automatic speech recognition and machine translation.

In this section, we'll explore an RNN model on a challenging task of language processing, guessing the next word in a sequence of text.

You can download the source code for this example here (official TensorFlow project GitHub page): *https://github.com/tensorflow/models/tree/master/tutorials/rnn/ptb*.

The files to download are as follows:

- ✓ ptb_word_lm.py: This file contains code to train the model on the PTB dataset
- ✓ reader.py: This file contains code to read the dataset

Dataset

The dataset used is the Penn Tree Bank (PTB) language modeling dataset that must be downloaded from Tomas Mikolov's webpage ***http://www.fit.vutbr.cz /~imikolov /rnnlm /simple-examples.tgz*** and then extracted in your data folder. This dataset consists of 929k training words, 73k validation words, and 82k test words. It has 10k words in its vocabulary including the end-of-sentence marker and a special symbol <unk> for rare words.

Generally speaking, a treebank is a collection of sentences collected according to a syntactic annotation scheme that makes machine readable information concerning the linguistic text structure.

Perplexity

The metric used to measure the goodness of the network is the so-called perplexity. The precise definition requires a lot of math, but it is roughly the average number of choices that the model may have after each word; if we consider spoken English, about one million words, currently the best network models have perplexity 247, a really big number of branching for each word.

PTB model

The PTB model is implemented through the PTBModel class that you can find in the ptb_word_lm.py file. Here we analyze the basic pseudo code.

The network model consists of a BasicLSTMCell cell:
lstm = rnn_cell.BasicLSTMCell(lstm_size)

The memory state of the network is initialized with a vector of zeros; the data is processed in a mini batch set of size batch_size:
state = tf.zeros([batch_size, lstm.state_size])

For each analyzed word, the probabilities for the continuations of the sentence are computed as follows:

probabilities = [ ]
for current_batch_of_words in words_in_dataset:

The value of state is updated after processing each batch of words:

output, state = lstm(current_batch_of_words, state)

The LSTM output is then used to make predictions on the next word:

logits = tf.matmul(output, softmax_w) + softmax_b
probabilities.append(tf.nn.softmax(logits))
loss += loss_function(probabilities, target_words)

The loss_function function minimizes the average negative log probability of the target words. It computes the average per-word perplexity.

Running the example

The PTB model can support small, medium, and large dataset configurations. The small model should be able to reach perplexity below 120 on the test set and the large one below 80, though it might take several hours to train.

We executed the model on the small size dataset. To do this, simply type in your command prompt the following: python ptb_word_lm --data_path=/tmp/simple-examples/data/ --model small. This is where you extracted the previously downloaded PTB dataset in /tmp/simple-examples/data/.

The preceding perplexity value after eight hours of training and 13 training epochs are as follows: Epoch:

1 Learning rate: 1.000
0.004 perplexity: 5263.762 speed: 391 wps
0.104 perplexity: 837.607 speed: 429 wps
0.204 perplexity: 617.207 speed: 442 wps
0.304 perplexity: 498.160 speed: 438 wps
0.404 perplexity: 430.516 speed: 436 wps
0.504 perplexity: 386.339 speed: 427 wps
0.604 perplexity: 348.393 speed: 431 wps
0.703 perplexity: 322.351 speed: 432 wps
0.803 perplexity: 301.630 speed: 431 wps
0.903 perplexity: 282.417 speed: 434 wps
Epoch: 1 Train Perplexity: 268.124
Epoch: 1 Valid Perplexity: 180.210
Epoch: 2 Learning rate: 1.000
0.004 perplexity: 209.082 speed: 448 wps
0.104 perplexity: 150.589 speed: 437 wps
0.204 perplexity: 157.965 speed: 436 wps
0.304 perplexity: 152.896 speed: 453 wps
0.404 perplexity: 150.299 speed: 458 wps
0.504 perplexity: 147.984 speed: 462 wps
0.604 perplexity: 143.367 speed: 462 wps
0.703 perplexity: 141.246 speed: 446 wps
0.803 perplexity: 139.299 speed: 436 wps
0.903 perplexity: 135.632 speed: 435 wps
Epoch: 2 Train Perplexity: 133.576

Epoch: 2 Valid Perplexity: 143.072

....

Epoch: 12 Learning rate: 0.008
0.004 perplexity: 57.011 speed: 347 wps
0.104 perplexity: 41.305 speed: 356 wps
0.204 perplexity: 45.136 speed: 356 wps
0.304 perplexity: 43.386 speed: 357 wps
0.404 perplexity: 42.624 speed: 358 wps
0.504 perplexity: 41.980 speed: 358 wps
0.604 perplexity: 40.549 speed: 357 wps
0.703 perplexity: 39.943 speed: 357 wps
0.803 perplexity: 39.287 speed: 358 wps
0.903 perplexity: 37.949 speed: 359 wps
Epoch: 12 Train Perplexity: 37.125
Epoch: 12 Valid Perplexity: 123.571
Epoch: 13 Learning rate: 0.004
0.004 perplexity: 56.576 speed: 365 wps
0.104 perplexity: 40.989 speed: 358 wps
0.204 perplexity: 44.809 speed: 358 wps
0.304 perplexity: 43.082 speed: 356 wps
0.404 perplexity: 42.332 speed: 356 wps
0.504 perplexity: 41.694 speed: 356 wps
0.604 perplexity: 40.275 speed: 357 wps
0.703 perplexity: 39.673 speed: 356 wps
0.803 perplexity: 39.021 speed: 356 wps
0.903 perplexity: 37.690 speed: 356 wps
Epoch: 13 Train Perplexity: 36.869
Epoch: 13 Valid Perplexity: 123.358
Test Perplexity: 117.171

6

Advanced TensorFlow Programming

Development of deep learning networks, especially when testing new models, may require rapid prototyping. For this reason, there have been developed several TensorFlow-based libraries, abstracting many programming concepts and providing higher-level building blocks. In this chapter, we'll give an overview of the libraries such as, Keras, Pretty Tensor, and TFLearn.

For each library, we'll describe its main characteristics, with an application example.

6.1 Introducing Keras

Keras is a minimalist, high-level neural networks library, capable of running on top of TensorFlow. It was developed with a focus on enabling easy and fast prototyping and experimentation. Keras runs on Python 2.7 or 3.5, and can seamlessly execute on GPUs and CPUs given the underlying frameworks. It is released under the MIT license.

Keras was developed and maintained by François Chollet, a Google engineer, following these design principles:

- ✓ **Modularity:** A model is understood as a sequence or a graph of the standalone, fully configurable modules that can be plugged together with as few restrictions as possible. Neural layers, cost functions, optimizers, initialization schemes, and activation functions are all standalone modules that can be combined to create new models.

- ✓ **Minimalism:** Each module must be short (few lines of code) and simple. The source code should be transparent upon the dirt reading.

- ✓ **Extensibility:** New modules are simple to add (as new classes and functions), and existing modules provide examples. To be able to easily create new modules allows for total expressiveness, making Keras suitable for advanced research.

- ✓ **Python:** No separate model configuration files in a declarative format. Models are described in Python code, which is compact, easier to debug, and allows for ease of extensibility.

The following screenshot shows the Keras homepage:

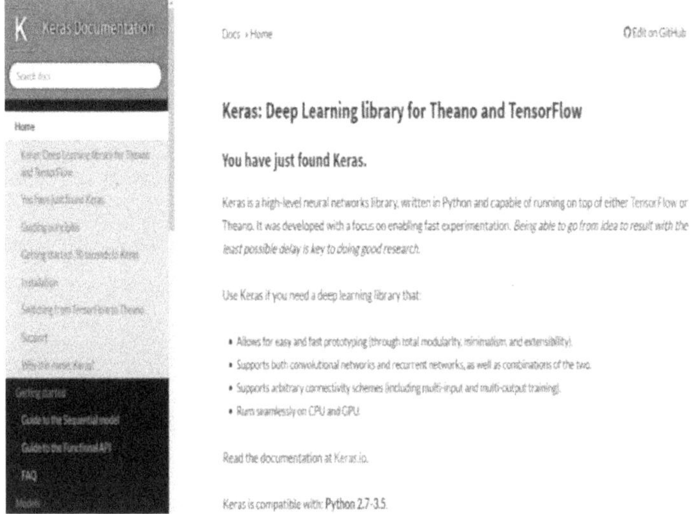

Figure 6.1 The Keras home page

6.2 Building deep learning models

The core data structure of Keras is a model, which is a way to organize layers. There are two types of model:

- ✓ Sequential: The main type of model. It is simply a linear stack of layers.
- ✓ Keras functional API: These are used for more complex architectures.

You define a sequential model as follows:

from keras.models import Sequential
model = Sequential()

Once a model is defined, you can add one or more layers. The stacking operation is provided by the add() statement: from keras.layers import Dense, Activation

For example, add a first fully connected NN layer and the Activation function:

model.add(Dense(output_dim=64, input_dim=100)
model.add(Activation("relu"))

Then add a second softmax layer:

model.add(Dense(output_dim=10))
model.add(Activation("softmax"))

If the model looks fine, you must compile the model by using the model.compile function, specifying the loss function and the optimizer function to be used:

```
model.compile(loss='categorical_crossentropy',\
optimzer='sgd',\
metrics=['accuracy'])
```

You may configure your optimizer. Keras tries to make programming reasonably simple, allowing the user to be fully in control when they need to be. Once compiled, the model must be fitted to the data: model.fit(X_train, Y_train, nb_epoch=5, batch_size=32

Alternatively, you can feed batches to your model manually:

```
model.train_on_batch(X_batch, Y_batch)
```

Once trained, you can use your model to make predictions on new data:

```
classes = model.predict_classes(X_test, batch_size=32)
proba = model.predict_proba(X_test, batch_size=32)
```

We can summarize the construction of deep learning models in Keras as follows:

- ✓ **Define your model:** Create a sequence and add layers.
- ✓ **Compile your model:** Specify loss functions and optimizers.
- ✓ **Fit your model:** Execute the model using data.
- ✓ **Evaluate the model:** Keep an evaluation of your training dataset.
- ✓ **Make predictions:** Use the model to generate predictions on new data.

The following figure depicts the preceding processes:

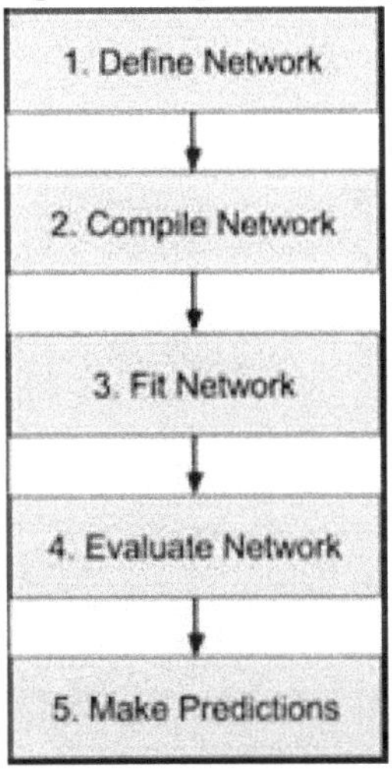

1. Define Network
2. Compile Network
3. Fit Network
4. Evaluate Network
5. Make Predictions

Figure 6.2 Keras programming model

6.3 Sentiment classification of movie reviews

Sentiment analysis is the capability to decipher the opinions contained in a written or spoken text. The main purpose of this technique is to identify the sentiment (or polarity) of a lexical expression, which may have a neutral, positive, or negative connotation.

The problem we want to resolve is the IMDB movie review sentiment classification problem. Each movie review is a variable sequence of words, and the sentiment (positive or negative) of each movie review must be classified.

This problem is very complex, because the sequences can vary in length; they can also be part of a large vocabulary of input symbols.

The solution requires the model to learn long-term dependencies between symbols in the input sequence.

The IMDB dataset contains 25,000 highly polarized movie reviews (good or bad) for training and the same amount again for testing. The data was collected by Stanford researchers, and was used in a 2011 paper, where a split of 50/50 of the data was used for training and testing. In this paper, an accuracy of 88.89% was achieved.

Once we define our problem, we are ready to develop an LSTM model to classify the sentiment of movie reviews. We can quickly develop an LSTM for the IMDB problem and achieve good accuracy.

Let's start off by importing the classes and functions required for this model, and initializing the random number generator to a constant value, to ensure we can easily reproduce the results:

```
import numpy
from keras.datasets import imdb
from keras.models import Sequential
from keras.layers import Dense
from keras.layers import LSTM
from keras.layers.embeddings import Embedding
from keras.preprocessing import sequence
numpy.random.seed(7)
```

We load the IMDB dataset. We are constraining the dataset to the top 5,000 words. We also split the dataset into training (50%) and testing (50%) sets.

Keras provides access to the IMDb dataset (http://www.imdb.com/interfaces) built-in. alternatively, you also can download the IMDB dataset from Kaggle website at https://www. kaggle.com/deepmatrix/imdb-5000-movie-dataset.

The imdb.load_data() function allows you to load the dataset in a format that is ready for use in neural network and deep learning models. The words have been replaced by integers, which indicate the ordered frequency of each word in the dataset. The sentences in each review are therefore comprised of a sequence of integers.

Here's the code:

```
top_words = 5000\
(X_train, y_train), (X_test, y_test) =\
imdb.load_data(nb_words=top_words)
```

Next, we need to truncate and pad the input sequences so that they are all the same length for modeling. The model will learn the zero values that carry no information because, although the sequences are not the same length in terms of content, same length vectors are required to perform the computation in Keras. The sequence length in each review varies, so we constrained each review to 500 words, truncating long reviews and padding the shorter reviews with zero values:

Let's see:

```
max_review_length = 500\
X_train = sequence.pad_sequences\
(X_train, maxlen=max_review_length)
X_test = sequence.pad_sequences\
(X_test, maxlen=max_review_length)
```

We can now define, compile, and fit our LSTM model.

To resolve the sentiment classification problem, we'll use the word embedding technique, which consists of representing words in a continuous vector space, that is, an area in which the words that are semantically similar are mapped in neighboring points. Word embedding is based on the distributional hypothesis, that is, the words that appear in a given context must share the same semantic meaning. Each movie review will then be mapped into a real vector domain, where the similarity between words, in terms of meaning, translates to closeness in the vector space. Keras provides a convenient way to convert positive integer representations of words into word embedding by an embedding layer.

Here, we define the length of the embedding vector and the model:

```
embedding_vector_length = 32
model = Sequential()
```

The first layer is the embedded layer, which uses 32 length vectors to represent each word:

```
model.add(Embedding(top_words,\
embedding_vector_length,\
input_length=max_review_length))
```

The next layer is the LSTM layer, with 100 memory units. Finally, because this is a classification problem, we use a Dense output layer with a single neuron and a sigmoid activation function to make 0 or 1 predictions for the two classes (good and bad) in the problem:

```
model.add(LSTM(100))
model.add(Dense(1, activation='sigmoid'))
```

Because it is a binary classification problem, the binary_crossentropy function is used as a loss function, while the optimizer function used here is the adam optimization algorithm (we also encountered it in a previous TensorFlow implementation):

```
model.compile(loss='binary_crossentropy',\
optimizer='adam',\
metrics=['accuracy'])
print(model.summary())
```

We fit only three epochs, because the problem quickly overfits. A batch size of 64 reviews is used to space out weight updates:

```
model.fit(X_train, y_train, \
validation_data=(X_test, y_test),\
nb_epoch=3,\
batch_size=64)
```

Then, we estimate the model's performance on unseen reviews:

```
scores = model.evaluate(X_test, y_test, verbose=0)
print("Accuracy: %.2f%%" % (scores[1]*100))
```

Running this example produces the following output:

```
Epoch 1/3
```

16750/16750
[==================================] - 107s - loss: 0.5570 - acc: 0.7149 Epoch 2/3
16750/16750
[==================================] - 107s - loss: 0.3530 - acc: 0.8577 Epoch 3/3
16750/16750
[==================================] - 107s - loss: 0.2559 - acc: 0.9019
Accuracy: 86.79%

You can see that this simple LSTM, with little tuning, achieves near state of the art results on the IMDB problem. Importantly, this is a template that you can use to apply LSTM networks to your own sequence classification problems.

6.4 Adding a convolutional layer

We can add one-dimensional CNN and max-pooling layers after the embedding layer, which will then feed the consolidated features to the LSTM.

Here is our embedding layer:

```
model = Sequential()
model.add(Embedding(top_words,\
embedding_vector_length,\
input_length=max_review_length))
```

We can apply a convolution layer with a small kernel filter (filter_length) of size 3, with 32 output features

```
(nb_filter):model.add(Conv1D(padding="same",
activation="relu", kernel_size=3,\ num_filter=32))
```

Next, we add a pooling layer; the size of the region to which max pooling is applied is equal to 2:

model.add(GlobalMaxPooling1D ())

The next layer is a LSTM layer, with 100 memory units:

model.add(LSTM(100))

The final layer is a Dense output layer, with a single neuron and a sigmoid activation function, to make 0 or 1 predictions for the two classes (good and bad) in the problem (that is, binary classification problem):

model.add(Dense(1, activation='sigmoid'))

Running this example provides the following output:

```
Epoch 1/3
16750/16750 [==============================] - 58s
- loss: 0.5186 - acc: 0.7263 Epoch 2/3
16750/16750 [==============================] - 58s
- loss: 0.2946 - acc: 0.8825 Epoch 3/3
16750/16750 [==============================] - 58s
- loss:
0.2291 - acc: 0.9126
Accuracy: 86.36%
```

The result obtained is a slight improvement on the accuracy of our model.

6.5 Pretty Tensor

Pretty Tensor allows the developer to wrap TensorFlow operations, to quickly chain any number of layers to define neural networks.

The following is a simple example of the Pretty Tensor capabilities. We wrap a standard TensorFlow object, pretty, into a library compatible object, then we feed it through three fully connected layers, to finally output a softmax distribution:

```
pretty = tf.placeholder([None, 784], tf.float32)
softmax = (prettytensor.wrap(examples)
.fully_connected(256, tf.nn.relu)
.fully_connected(128, tf.sigmoid)
.fully_connected(64, tf.tanh)
.softmax(10))
```

The Pretty Tensor installation is very simple; just use the pip installer:

```
sudo pip install prettytensor
```

6.6 Digit classifier

In this example, we'll define and train either a two-layer model or a convolutional model in the style of

LeNet 5:

```
from six.moves import xrange
import tensorflow as tf
import prettytensor as pt
```

```
from prettytensor.tutorial import data_utils
tf.app.flags.DEFINE_string(
'save_path', None, 'Where to save the model checkpoints.')
FLAGS = tf.app.flags.FLAGS
BATCH_SIZE = 50
EPOCH_SIZE = 60000 // BATCH_SIZE
TEST_SIZE = 10000 // BATCH_SIZE
```

Since we are feeding our data as numpy arrays, we need to create placeholders in the graph. These must then be fed using the feed dict.

```
image_placeholder = tf.placeholder\
(tf.float32, [BATCH_SIZE, 28, 28, 1])
labels_placeholder = tf.placeholder\
(tf.float32, [BATCH_SIZE, 10])
tf.app.flags.DEFINE_string('model', 'full',
'Choose one of the models, either
full or conv')
FLAGS = tf.app.flags.FLAGS
```

We created the following function, multilayer_fully_connected. The first two layers are fully connected (100 neurons), and the final layer is a softmax result layer. Note that the chaining layer is a very simple operation:

```
def multilayer_fully_connected(images, labels):
images = pt.wrap(images)
with pt.defaults_scope\
(activation_fn=tf.nn.relu,l2loss=0.00001):
return (images.flatten().\
fully_connected(100).\
fully_connected(100).\
softmax_classifier(10, labels))
```

In the following, we'll build a multilayer convolutional network; the architecture is similar to that defined in LeNet 5. Please change this to experiment with other architectures:

```
def lenet5(images, labels):
images = pt.wrap(images)
with pt.defaults_scope\
(activation_fn=tf.nn.relu, l2loss=0.00001):
return (images.conv2d(5, 20).\
max_pool(2, 2).\
conv2d(5, 50).\
max_pool(2, 2). \
flatten().\
fully_connected(500).\
softmax_classifier(10, labels))
```

Since we are feeding our data as numpy arrays, we need to create placeholders in the graph. These must then be fed using the feed dict:

```
def main(_=None):
image_placeholder = tf.placeholder\
(tf.float32, [BATCH_SIZE, 28, 28, 1])
labels_placeholder = tf.placeholder\
(tf.float32, [BATCH_SIZE, 10])
```

Depending on FLAGS.model, we may have a two-layer classifier or a convolutional classifier, previously defined:

```
def main(_=None):
if FLAGS.model == 'full':
result = multilayer_fully_connected\
(image_placeholder, labels_placeholder)
elif FLAGS.model == 'conv':
```

```
result = lenet5(image_placeholder, labels_placeholder)
else:
raise ValueError\
('model must be full or conv: %s' % FLAGS.model)
```

Then we define the accuracy function for the evaluated classifier:

```
accuracy = result.softmax.evaluate_classifier\
(labels_placeholder,phase=pt.Phase.test)
```

Next, we build the training and test sets:

```
train_images, train_labels = data_utils.mnist(training=True)
test_images, test_labels = data_utils.mnist(training=False)
```

We will use a gradient descent optimizer procedure and apply it to the graph. The pt.apply_optimizer function adds regularization losses and sets up a step counter:

```
optimizer = tf.train.GradientDescentOptimizer(0.01)\
train_op = pt.apply_optimizer
(optimizer,losses=[result.loss])
```

We can set save_path in the running session to automatically checkpoint every so often. Otherwise, at the end of the session, the model will be lost:

```
runner = pt.train.Runner(save_path=FLAGS.save_path)
with tf.Session():
for epoch in xrange(10):
Shuffle the training data:
train_images, train_labels =\
data_utils.permute_data\
((train_images, train_labels))
```

```
runner.train_model(train_op,result.\
loss,EPOCH_SIZE,\
feed_vars=(image_placeholder, \
labels_placeholder),\
feed_data=pt.train.\
feed_numpy(BATCH_SIZE,\
train_images,\
train_labels),\
print_every=100)
classification_accuracy = runner.evaluate_model\
(accuracy,\
TEST_SIZE,\
feed_vars=(image_placeholder,\
labels_placeholder), \
feed_data=pt.train.\
feed_numpy(BATCH_SIZE,\
test_images,\
test_labels))
print('epoch' , epoch + 1)
print('accuracy', classification_accuracy )
if __name__ == '__main__':
tf.app.run()
```

Running this example provides the following output:

```
>>>
Extracting /tmp/data/train-images-idx3-ubyte.gz
Extracting tmp/data/train-labels-idx1-ubyte.gz
Extracting /tmp/data/t10k-images-idx3-ubyte.gz
Extracting /tmp/data/t10k-labels-idx1-ubyte.gz
epoch =        1
Accuracy       [0.8994]
epoch =        2
Accuracy       [0.91549999]
```

epoch = 3
Accuracy [0.92259997]
epoch = 4
Accuracy [0.92760003]
epoch = 5
Accuracy [0.9303]
epoch = 6
Accuracy [0.93870002]
epoch = 7
epoch = 8
Accuracy [0.94700003]
epoch = 9
Accuracy [0.94910002]
epoch = 10
Accuracy [0.94980001]

7
Reinforcement Learning

Reinforcement Learning is based on an interesting psychological theory: Applying a reward immediately after the occurrence of a response increases its probability of reoccurring, while providing punishment after the response will decrease the probability (Thorndike, 1911).

A reward, received immediately after the execution of a correct behavior, increases the likelihood that this behavior will be repeated; while, following an undesired behavior, the application of a punishment decreases the likelihood of that error reocurring. Therefore, once a goal has been established, Reinforcement Learning seeks to maximize the rewards received, to achieve the designated goal.

7.1 Basic concepts of Reinforcement Learning

Reinforcement Learning (RL) aims to create systems that will learn and, at the same time, adapt to changes in the environment in which they are located, using a reward that is assigned to each action performed. Software systems that process information in this way are called intelligent agents.

These agents decide to take an action based on the following:

- ✓ State of the system
- ✓ Learning algorithm used

To change the system state and maximize its long term rewards, and agent selects the action to be performed by continuously monitoring its environment. To obtain a large reward and, therefore, optimize the Reinforcement Learning procedure, the agent must prefer actions that, in the past, have produced a good reward.

The actions are discovered, proving those never selected first. Therefore, the agent must exploit what it already knows, both to obtain the maximum reward, and also to explore and select the best actions for the future.

To do that, the agent should try a variety of actions and progressively favor those which seem to be the best. It then proceeds stochastically, where every action must be tried many times to get a reliable estimate of the expected reward.

Here, we describe the four main sub-elements of a Reinforcement Learning system. The first one is the policy, which defines the way in which the agent must behave at a given time. In other words, a policy is a mapping between the states perceived by the environment and the actions to take when the agent is in those specific states. The policy is the heart of a Reinforcement Learning agent, because it determines the behaviour that the agent must take.

The second main sub-element defines the goal of a Reinforcement Learning problem. This is the reward function. Each state is mapped with its own reward, indicating the degree of desire to be in that state. As mentioned previously, the goal of a Reinforcement Learning agent will be to maximize the total reward that it receives in the long run.

The third main sub-element is the value function. This function specifies what is good in the long run. In other words, the value of a state is the total amount of reward that an agent can expect to accumulate for the future, starting from that state. While the rewards determine an immediate desirability of the states, the values indicate the long-term desirability of states, taking into account the states that may follow and the available rewards in those states. The value function is specified with respect to the chosen policy.

During the learning phase, an agent tries actions that determine the states with the highest value, because these actions will get the best amount of reward in the long run. While the rewards are derived directly from the environment, the values must be constantly estimated, observing an agent throughout its lifetime.

In fact, the most important component of a Reinforcement Learning algorithm is a method for efficiently estimating the values.

Finally, we have the last main sub-element, which is the environment (or model). This is an agent internal representation that stimulates the behavior of the environment. For example, given a state and an action, the model predicts what the next resulting state and next reward will be.

The following figure summarizes the Reinforcement Learning cycle:

Figure 7.1 Reinforcement learning cycle

An agent receives sensory information about the environment's state. Based on this information and the defined policies, the agent performs an action in the environment. This results in a reward signal. Unlike the sensory information, which may be a large feature vector, or the action, which may also have many components, the reward is a single real-valued scalar; a number.

In addition, the performed action changes the environment, leading it in a new state, where the agent can perform a new action, and so on. The goal of learning is the maximization of the reward received, that is, this does not mean maximizing the immediate reward, but the cumulative reward received over time.

7.2 Q-learning algorithm

Solving a Reinforcement Learning problem during the learning process estimates an evaluation function. This function must be able to assess, through the sum of the rewards, the convenience or, otherwise, a policy. The basic idea of Q-learning is that the algorithm learns the optimal evaluation function on the whole space of states and actions (SxA). The so-called Q-function provides a match in the form $Q: S \times A => V$, where V is the value of future rewards of an action, a Î A, executed in the state s Î S.

Once it has learned the optimal function, Q, the agent will of course be able to recognize what action will lead to the highest future reward in a s state. One of the most used examples for implementing the Q-learning algorithm involves the use of a table. Each cell of the table is a value, $Q(s; a)= V$, initialized to 0.

The agent can perform any action a Î A, where A is the total set of actions known by the agent. The basic idea of the algorithm is the training rule, which updates a table element, Q (s; a).

The algorithm follows these basic steps:

Initialize Q (s; a) arbitrarily
Repeat (for each episode)
Initialize s
Repeat (for each step of episode):
Choose an action a I A from s I S using policy
derived from Q
Take an action a, observe r, s'
Q(s; a) - Q(s; a) + a .(r + g. max Q(s'; a) - Q(s; a))
s' :s- s'
Until s is terminal

The parameters used in the Q-value update process are as follows: a is the learning rate, set between 0 and 1. Setting it to 0 means that the Q-values are never updated, hence nothing is learned. Setting a high value, such as 0.9, means that learning can occur quickly. g is the discount factor, also set between 0 and 1. This models the fact that future rewards are worth less than immediate rewards.

Mathematically, the discount factor needs to be set to less than 0 for the algorithm to converge. max Q(s'; a) is the maximum reward attainable in the state following the current one, that is, the reward for taking the optimal action thereafter.

For better understanding, we have depicted the algorithm in the following figure:

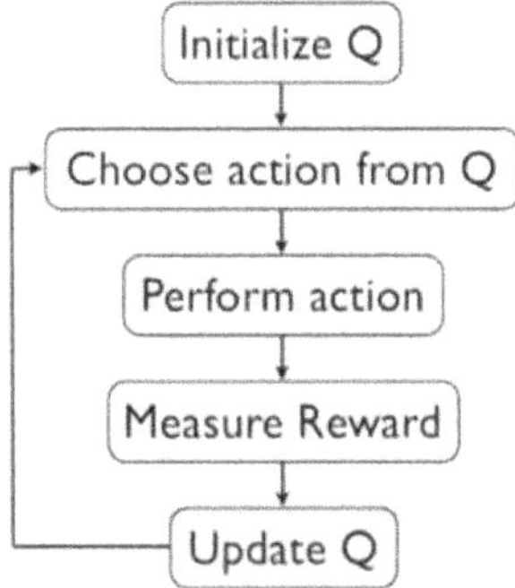

Figure 7.2 Q-learning algorithm

7.3 Introducing the OpenAI Gym framework

To implement a Q-learning algorithm we'll use the OpenAI Gym framework, which is a TensorFlow compatible toolkit for developing and comparing Reinforcement Learning algorithms.

OpenAI Gym consists of two main parts:

The Gym open source library: A collection of problems and environments that can be used to test Reinforcement Learning algorithms. All these environments have a shared interface, allowing you to write RL algorithms.

The OpenAI Gym service: A site and API allowing people to meaningfully compare the performance of their trained agents.

To get started, you'll need to have Python 2.7 or Python 3.5. To install Gym, use the pip installer:

sudo pip install gym.

Once installed, you can list Gym's environments as follows:

>>>from gym import envs
>>>print(envs.registry.all())

The output list is very long; the following is just an excerpt:

[EnvSpec(PredictActionsCartpole-v0),
EnvSpec(AsteroidsramDeterministic-v0),
EnvSpec(Asteroids-ramDeterministic-v3),
EnvSpec(Gopher-ramDeterministic-v3),
EnvSpec(Gopher-ramDeterministic-v0),
EnvSpec(DoubleDunk-ramDeterministic-v3),
EnvSpec(DoubleDunk-ramDeterministic-v0),
EnvSpec(Carnival-v0),
EnvSpec(FrozenLake-v0),.....,
EnvSpec(SpaceInvaders-ram-v3),
EnvSpec(CarRacing-v0), EnvSpec(SpaceInvaders-ram-v0), ...,
EnvSpec(Kangaroo-v0)]

Each EnvSpec defines a task to resolve, for example, the FrozenLake-v0 representation is given in the following figure. The agent controls the movement of a character in a 4x4 grid world (see the following figure). Some tiles of the grid are walkable, and others lead to the agent falling into the water. Additionally, the movement direction of the agent is uncertain, and only partially depends on the chosen direction. The agent is rewarded for finding a walkable path to a goal tile:

Figure 7.3 A representation of the FrozenLake v0 grid word

The surface shown previously is described using a grid, such as the following:

SFFF (S: starting point, safe)
FHFH (F: frozensurface, safe)
FFFH (H: hole, fall to yourdoom)
HFFG (G: goal, where the frisbee islocated)

The episode ends when we reach the goal or fall in a hole. We receive a reward of one for reaching the goal, and zero otherwise.

7.4 Implementing FrozenLake-v0

Here we report a basic Q-learning implementation for the FrozenLake-v0 problem.

Import the following two basic libraries:

import gym
import numpyasnp

Then, we load the FrozenLake-v0 environment:

environment = gym.make('FrozenLake-v0')

Then, we build the Q-learning table; it has the dimensions SxA, where S is the dimension of the observation space, S, while A is the dimension of the action space, A:

```
S = environment.observation_space.n
A = environment.action_space.n
```

The FrozenLake environment provides a state for each block, and four actions (that is, the four directions of movement), giving us a 16x4 table of Q-values to initialize:

```
Q = np.zeros([S,A])
```

Then, we define the a parameter for the training rule and the discount g factor:

```
alpha = .85
gamma = .99
```

We fix the total number of episodes (trials):

```
num_episodes = 2000
```

Then, we initialize the rList, where we'll append the cumulative reward to evaluate the algorithm's score:

```
rList = [ ]
```

Finally, we start the Q-learning cycle:

```
for i in range(num_episodes):
```

Initialize the environment and other parameters:

```
s = environment.reset()
cumulative_reward = 0
d = False
j = 0
while j < 99:
j+=1
```

Randomically, we take an action from the space A:

```
a = np.argmax(Q[s,:] + np.random.randn(1,A)*(1./(i+1)))
```

We evaluate the action, a, by the function, environment.step(), getting the reward and the state s1:

```
s1,reward,d,_ = env.step(a)
```

Update the Q(s; a) table with the training rule:

```
Q[s,a] = Q[s,a] + alpha*(reward + gamma*np.max(Q[s1,:]) -
Q[s,a])
cumulative_reward += reward
```

Set the state for the next learning cycle:

```
s = s1
if d == True:
break
rList.append(cumulative_reward)
```

Print the score over time and the resulting Q-table:

print "Score over time: " + str(sum(rList)/num_episodes)
print "Final Q-TableValues"
print Q

The average reward is about 0.54 over 100 consecutive trials as shown in the following figure:

```
[2017-03-23 12:22:49,913] Making new env: FrozenLake-v0
Score over time: 0.3585
Final Q-Table Values
[[  4.90034838e-03   1.23733520e-02   5.04857351e-01   1.18572787e-02]
 [  6.14009765e-04   1.34354386e-03   1.39327124e-03   5.88345699e-01]
 [  2.42003179e-03   2.53712381e-03   1.27103632e-03   3.36417875e-01]
 [  1.60332674e-03   6.60331077e-04   6.50987843e-04   1.96388199e-01]
 [  6.38172447e-01   1.23434831e-03   1.35672865e-03   8.99709408e-05]
 [  0.00000000e+00   0.00000000e+00   0.00000000e+00   0.00000000e+00]
 [  1.78445198e-01   1.27421388e-04   2.70432817e-05   7.55201005e-12]
 [  0.00000000e+00   0.00000000e+00   0.00000000e+00   0.00000000e+00]
 [  5.85462465e-05   1.52400799e-03   6.22678642e-05   3.00741687e-01]
 [  3.15488045e-03   6.66874039e-02   0.00000000e+00   4.21513681e-04]
 [  7.99666157e-01   9.87928455e-04   2.11361272e-04   2.11179559e-04]
 [  0.00000000e+00   0.00000000e+00   0.00000000e+00   0.00000000e+00]
 [  0.00000000e+00   0.00000000e+00   0.00000000e+00   0.00000000e+00]
 [  1.20525081e-04   0.00000000e+00   9.20956992e-01   0.00000000e+00]
 [  0.00000000e+00   0.00000000e+00   9.91561828e-01   0.00000000e+00]
 [  0.00000000e+00   0.00000000e+00   0.00000000e+00   0.00000000e+00]]
```

Figure 7.4 A representation of the FrozenLake v0 grid word

7.5 Q-learning with TensorFlow

In the previous example, we saw how it is relatively simple, using a 16x4 grid, to update the Q-table at each step of the learning process. It is easy to imagine that the use of this table can serve for simple problems, but in real-world problems, we need a more sophisticated mechanism to update the system state. This is the point where deep learning steps in. Neural networks are exceptionally good at coming up with good features for highly structured data.

In this final section, we'll look at how to manage a Q-function with a neural network, which takes the state and action as input, and outputs the corresponding Q-value.

To do that, we'll build a one layer network that takes the state, encoded in a [1x16] vector, which learns the best move (action), mapping the possible actions in a vector of length four.

In the following, we describe our TensorFlow-based implementation of a Q-learning neural network for the FrozenLake-v0 problem.

Import all the libraries with the help of the following code:

```
import gym
import numpy as np
import random
import tensorflow as tf
import matplotlib.pyplot as plt
```

To install matplotlib, you should execute the following commands on terminal:

```
$ apt-cache search python3-matplotlib
$ sudo apt-get install python3-matplotlib
```

Load and set the environment to test:

```
env = gym.make('FrozenLake-v0')
```

The input network is a state, encoded in a tensor of shape [1,16]. For this reason, we define the inputs1 placeholder:

```
inputs1 = tf.placeholder(shape=[1,16],dtype=tf.float32)
```

The network weights are initially chosen randomly by the tf.random_uniform function:

W = tf.Variable(tf.random_uniform([16,4],0,0.01))

The network output is given by the product of the inputs1 placeholder and the weights:

Qout = tf.matmul(inputs1,W)

The argmax evaluated on Qout will give the predicted value:

predict = tf.argmax(Qout,1)

The best move (Qtarget) is encoded in a [1,4] tensor shape:

Qtarget = tf.placeholder(shape=[1,4],dtype=tf.float32)

Next, we must define a loss function to optimize for the backpropagation procedure. The loss function is as follows:

$$loss = \sum(Q\text{-}target - Q)^2$$

Where the difference between the current predicted Q-values and the target value is computed, and the gradients are passed through the network:

loss = tf.reduce_sum(tf.square(Qtarget- Qout))

The optimizing function, is the well-known GradientDescentOptimizer:

```
trainer = tf.train.GradientDescentOptimizer(learning_rate=0.1)
updateModel = trainer.minimize(loss)
```

Reset and initialize the computational graph:

```
tf.reset_default_graph()
init = tf.global_variables_initializer()
```

Following this, we set the parameter for the Q-learning training procedure:

```
gamma = .99
e = 0.1
num_episodes = 6000
jList = [ ]
rList - [ ]
```

We carry out the running session, in which the network will have to learn the best possible sequence of moves:

```
with tf.Session() as sess:
sess.run(init)
for i in range(num_episodes):
s = env.reset()
rAll = 0
d = False
j = 0
while j < 99:
j+=1
```

The input state is used here to feed the network:

```
a,allQ = sess.run([predict,Qout],\
feed_dict=\
{inputs1:np.identity(16)[s:s+1]})
```

A random state is chosen from the output tensor, a:

```
if np.random.rand(1) < e:
a[0] = env.action_space.sample()
```

Evaluate the action, a[0], using the function env.step(), obtaining the reward, r, and the state, s1:

```
s1,r,d,_ = env.step(a[0])
```

This new state s1 is used to update the Q-tensor:

```
Q1 = sess.run(Qout,feed_dict=\
{inputs1:np.identity(16)[s1:s1+1]})
maxQ1 = np.max(Q1)
targetQ = allQ
targetQ[0,a[0]] = r + y*maxQ1
```

Of course, the weights must be updated for the backpropagation procedure:

```
_,W1 = sess.run([updateModel,W],\
feed_dict=\
{inputs1:np.identity(16)[s:s+1],nextQ:targetQ})
```

The rAll parameter, here, defines the total reward that will be incremented during the session. Let's recall that the goal of a

Reinforcement Learning agent will be to maximize the total reward that it receives in the long run:

```
rAll += r
```

Update the state of the environment for the next step:

```
s = s1
if d == True:
e = 1./((i/50) + 10)
break
jList.append(j)
rList.append(rAll)
```

When the computation ends, the percent of successful episodes will be displayed:

```
print "Percent of succesfulepisodes: " +\
str(sum(rList)/num_episodes) + "%"
```

Running the model, you should have a result like the following, which can be improved by tuning the network parameters:

```
>>>
[2017-03-23 12:36:19,986] Making new env: FrozenLake-v0
Percent of successful episodes: 0.558%
>>>
```

www.ingramcontent.com/pod-product-compliance
Ingram Content Group UK Ltd.
Pitfield, Milton Keynes, MK11 3LW, UK
UKHW062311290726
14090UKWH00018B/1008